Praise for *The Marriage Knot*

The Marriage Knot is a must-read from my good friends Ron and Jody Zappia. They put it all out there for you to learn, grow, and receive healing from your pain. Through their life experiences, they have given us seven choices that we all need to practice to make sure that our marriages do not unravel. The sharing from Jody's heart at the end of each chapter is such an added bonus. These words will encourage and provoke you. Love it!

WILFREDO DE JESÚS
Senior Pastor of New Life Covenant Church, Chicago, IL

With so many marriages coming apart these days, it's hard to find people who believe they should stay together at all, let alone someone with fresh practical insights on how that can happen for you. Pastor Ron Zappia and his wife, Jody, know how to tie and retie a life of love that lasts. Ron and Jody are students of God's Word and the marriage lessons here are proven first in their own marriage then in the lives of many others. For you or someone you know whose marriage is unraveling, Ron Zappia has the right message at the right moment. Learn how to hold it together and love marriage more than you ever have–in *The Marriage Knot*.

JAMES AND KATHY MACDONALD
James is Senior Pastor of Harvest Bible Chapel, teacher for Walk in the Word, and author of many books, including *Act Like Men*

With authenticity and transp[...] appia show a path to a better marri[...] se, and Donna and I have learned fr[...] rney. Now, in *The Marriage Knot: [...] ther*, you can get the wisdom you need to build a marriage that lasts.

ED STETZER
Billy Graham Distinguished Chair, Wheaton College

If authenticity and hope is a hit, this book is a grand slam. Ron reveals the pain of broken lives and the power of redemption. He and Jody share their story as proof that Jesus can heal, tie two people's hearts together, and change lives–even yours. Grab their coattails of faith and run the race!

KARL CLAUSON
Host of Moody Radio's *Karl and Crew Mornings*, WMBI 90.1 FM, Chicago, IL; Lead Pastor of 180 Chicago

There is no doubt in my mind that this book will help many marriages. The reason is simple: it explains and illustrates the foundational issues that bring harmony and understanding to our marital relationships. Every marriage has room for growth, and this book is destined to accelerate our learning curve.

ERWIN W. LUTZER
Pastor Emeritus of The Moody Church in Chicago, IL; bestselling author

There aren't many books about marriage that I would read and recommend, but this one, *The Marriage Knot*, grabbed my attention from the very beginning and surprised me throughout. Ron's genuineness and authenticity shine throughout the book, and his biblical insight gives authority to the stories he tells. There is no marriage, whether you're engaged to wed or married fifty years, that won't benefit from this well-written book. This book is great because it's written by a wonderful fellow that is dedicated to our Lord, to his wife, and to the institution of marriage. Thanks, Ron . . . you've outdone yourself on this book!

MARK GREGSTON
Host of *Parenting Today's Teens* Radio

the marriage knot

the marriage knot

7

Choices That Keep Couples Together

RON & JODY ZAPPIA

MOODY PUBLISHERS

CHICAGO

Edited by Elizabeth Cody Newenhuyse
Interior design: Puckett Smartt
Author photo: Molly Grace Photography
Cover design: Stephen Vosloo
Cover photo of knot copyright © 2018 by dbphotos/Adobe Stock (75986199). All rights reserved.

ISBN: 978-0-8024-1845-6

We hope you enjoy this book from Moody Publishers. Our goal is to provide high-quality, thought-provoking books and products that connect truth to your real needs and challenges. For more information on other books and products that will help you with all your important relationships, go to www.moodypublishers.com or write to:

Moody Publishers
820 N. La Salle Boulevard
Chicago, IL 60610

1 3 5 7 9 10 8 6 4 2

Printed in the United States of America

*To my best friend and amazing wife, Jody.
Thank you for your unwavering
and unrelenting commitment to build
our life and marriage on the Rock with me.*

Contents

Introduction

f I asked you to tie a knot, what kind of knot would it be? If you're a boater, it would probably be a reef knot. If you're a fisherman, it would most likely be a blood knot. If a rock climber, it would certainly be a figure eight or a bowline. Or if you're inexperienced like I am, with no scouting background at all, you would probably tie the knot like you tie your shoes every day.

Either way, it wouldn't matter—because, as everyone knows, no matter the type, all knots loosen over time. Eventually, left unattended and unchecked, the knot comes undone. That same principle is true of the bond of marriage. The marriage covenant begins as a strong, tightly tied knot of commitment, love, devotion, and affection. Over time, however, left to itself the knot loosens; if left too long, it can completely unravel.

In this book I present seven personal choices a husband and wife can make to tighten and strengthen their marriage. Why? Because the truth is this: it's way easier to tie the marriage knot together at the altar on that perfect (but expensive) wedding day than it is to do the hard work of tightening it each day, week, month, and year. These seven choices are the choices that my wife, Jody, and I have learned and labored over to help keep our marriage from unraveling. Admittedly, there have been times when we've seen the marriage knot as a beautiful bow to be adored, and other times, if we're being completely honest, it felt more like a noose around our necks strangling the life out of us. I'm just keeping it real and raw, as marriage has been the crucible that God used to refine us, define us, and form us into the man, the woman, and the couple that He wants us to be.

Please take note: These principles didn't come from our own ingenuity and creativity or from some fictitious couple living down the street who everyone thinks has that perfect marriage. They come directly from the Bible and represent the commitments you and I can make to tighten the marriage knot and make certain that bond of commitment and affection remains strong.

Since the beginning, the knot has been God's idea and ideal for ensuring a strong, lifelong marriage relationship that is rooted in Him.

God's Vision for the Bond of Marriage

Wise Solomon described the importance of a strong bond for any meaningful and lasting relationship—especially marriage. Here's how Solomon envisioned it:

> Two are better than one,
>> because they have a good return for their labor:
> If either of them falls down,
>> one can help the other up.
> But pity anyone who falls
>> and has no one to help them up.
> Also, if two lie down together, they will keep warm.
>> But how can one keep warm alone?
> Though one may be overpowered,
>> two can defend themselves.
> A cord of three strands is not quickly broken.
> (Eccl. 4:9–12 NIV)

The principles laid out in that Bible passage have certainly proven true in my own marriage. Jody and I have known each other for thirty-five years. We met in middle school, if you can believe that! It was so long ago, but I remember the day she asked me for twenty cents to make a phone call. Yes, that was long before smartphones, texting, and even pagers—anybody remember those? At the urging of a friend she said, "Ron, do you have twenty cents I can borrow for a phone call to my parents to pick me up?" She was stranded, a damsel in distress. Here was my chance to be her knight in shining armor—in the eighth grade! That was literally our first conversation. I must admit I was more than glad that she asked as she rocked those Levi's cords like no other. I still tell her that today, by the way. Certainly, I gave her the money. The next day she walked up to me as my heart started beating faster and tried to pay me back. But, trying super hard to impress her, I responded, "Oh no, I'll have none of that—you don't ever need to pay me back." If you asked Jody about that twenty cents today, she would tell you she's been paying it back ever since and that it was the most expensive call she's ever made! Seriously, though, I had no idea that a couple of dimes would mark the beginning of a lasting relationship with my best friend and future wife.

That conversation in the hallway of our middle school began a friendship that became a relationship that eventually led us to tie the knot a couple years after college. It was our marriage knot, and yet, it wasn't until that knot was retied years later in Christ and rooted in the truth of God's Word that it became the strong bond of marriage that it is today. And from Solomon's words, we've discovered some practical principles that have guided us ever since.

We are united in marriage to accomplish more

In God's eyes, two are better than one. Imagine you have a yard covered with leaves. I live in the Midwest, and we have two huge trees in our front yard, so this is a reality for us—especially in October. As winter approaches, the yard needs to be raked. And is it just my kids, or are yours never around during leaf-raking season either? Just kidding, we have great kids. But here's the question: Would you rather have one person or two for that task of raking the leaves? Of course, you'd prefer two or three or four if possible. Why? Because you always accomplish more together. (Plus, raking alone is a pain!)

The same is true in marriage. In marriage, a husband and wife complement one another and become better together than they are apart as they, in a sense, complete each other. They work together to sharpen each other, smooth out the rough edges, and grow into the best versions of themselves.

We're joined in marriage to get the most out of life. That's God's heart, and His gracious desire is that we wouldn't do life alone, but rather that we would be in partnership together seeing more, enjoying more, and accomplishing more as we truly are better together. That's why we need each other.

We are united in marriage to lift up each other

Solomon wrote: "For if they fall, one will lift up his fellow. But woe to him who is alone when he falls and has not another to lift him up!" (Eccl. 4:10)

A strong relationship represents a mutual commitment to help each other in tough times. We are called to lift each other from despair, discouragement, defeat, even grief. And that lifting includes encouragement, which can come in so many forms and in different ways. If you haven't fallen yet, you will. It's not a matter of if; it's a matter of when. We all fall. Some of us are, unfortunately, continuing to fall into the same holes day after day, month after month, and year after year, unable to move forward to experience true lasting change. What do we do?

We need each other to provide a hand to hold on to, a shoulder to cry on, and an embrace to rely on during these difficult times. It's of critical importance for us to walk shoulder to shoulder, not back to back or even side to side in order to strengthen, support, and encourage each other through trying times. Being in ministry now for so many years, I've witnessed people fall in some of the most common yet devastating and painful ways. In fact, I've identified seven of the most ordinary ways people fall.

1. The Physical Fall

The first kind of fall that Solomon addresses is the physical fall. If your spouse falls and sprains an ankle or breaks a leg, he or she would need help getting around for several weeks, at least. I remember when my dad had back surgery and was confined to a wheelchair for an extended period. My mom had to push him around and help him as he struggled to get out of the wheelchair, gain balance, and begin to walk again. She was literally giving him a hand to hold on to and, in turn, he was relying on her. It's a perfect application of Solomon's words. They were lifting up each other in a beautiful picture of how God designed marriage to work.

2. The Financial Fall

Some people experience a financial fall. I remember a couple we became friends with who had experienced great financial success in the business world that resulted in the big house, boat, and vacation home, only to lose it all in a lawsuit that seemed very unfair and unjust. Maybe you've been there in your life. One day your finances are strong and you don't have a care in the world. Then, in a moment, tragedy strikes and you're in a financial free fall. When that happens, we need one another to make some hard decisions and pick up the pieces together.

3. The Relational Fall

Another is the relational fall. A relational fall occurs when one person hurts someone else. It might be within the marital relationship or in another important one such as a family member or close friend. Maybe there is a hurt that requires some assistance or intervention. There are many degrees and types of relational falls, and we all experience them. When we do, we need another person to walk with us through the pain and perhaps help us facilitate forgiveness in love. As I've navigated these waters, Jody has been so helpful to me in understanding people to a much greater degree—their thoughts, their emotions, their responses, and their actions.

4. The Moral Fall

Sadly, many marriages break down because of moral failure. This is when we do things the Bible says not to do—when the marriage covenant is broken because either the husband or wife commits a moral lapse. We become vulnerable to this when we make a series of compromises contrary to what the Bible teaches. When these behaviors go unchecked or unconfessed and culminate in marital unfaithfulness, the marriage knot unravels. We, and those closest to us, suffer untold consequences.

Yet even such a serious breach of trust is not beyond repair. The most painful situations can be restored as mature and wise godly counsel is sought and followed. More about that later!

5. The Emotional Fall

All of us are susceptible to emotional falls. The Bible includes numerous examples of godly people who struggled with their emotions. The prophet Elijah told God he wanted to die (1 Kings 19:1-4). Jonah did, too (Jonah 1:12). Many of David's psalms also described the strong emotions he experienced (Pss. 42-43). When someone experiences an emotional fall, a nonjudgmental, listening ear goes a long way, especially one that is committed to understanding and seeing you through it.

6. The Spiritual Fall

Spiritual falls occur in marriages when we stop growing in our relationship with God. I often say there is no coasting in neutral as a

Christian. Here's a backswing thought for every follower of Christ: if you are not going forward, you are going backward. There are no holding patterns in the Christian life. Sometimes one of us is growing stronger in relationship with God while the other is trapped in bitterness or doubt or crippled in fear. Spiritual falls require God's help and a plan to move forward, to pursue God in obedience and faith with the help of others.

7. The Repeated Fall

The seventh kind of fall can be the most severe: repeated falls. It's when someone continues stumbling over the same thing, lapsing back into past patterns of sinfulness, or even addictions. No one is immune to these kinds of falls in life. How do we get through them? God has designed us to get through such times together. We are here to help each other, to walk in a different direction, and to respond in a new healthy way.

But too often we live in isolation. In fact, isolation has become the curse of our age. You can be in a marriage relationship and still experience terrible periods of loneliness and despair. Over time, if unattended to, the marriage knot comes loose. The relationship grows cold because it has grown silent. It doesn't grow cold before it grows silent. Marriage goes silent and then grows cold.

God Himself said it: it is not good for man to be alone (Gen. 2:18). That's never been part of His plan. He created us to be in relationship with Him and with each other.

We are united in marriage to provide for each other

God designed marriage to be an experience of mutual provision. Solomon wrote: "Likewise, two people lying close together can keep each other warm. But how can one be warm alone?" (Eccl. 4:11 NLT).

Solomon wrote those powerful words long before electricity and the advent of modern conveniences that most people enjoy today. In Solomon's day, homes were heated by fires, especially at night.

17

Warmth was important. Keeping each other warm in bed at night was a compellingly clear picture of mutual provision.

We are united in marriage to protect each other

Another reason for relationship is mutual protection.

> A person standing alone can be attacked and defeated, but two can stand back-to-back and conquer. (Eccl. 4:12a NLT)

In God's eyes, relationships, especially in marriage, provide protection. On our tenth wedding anniversary, Jody and I traveled to Monterey, California. One morning we were biking along the shoreline and noticed that the ocean was alive and powerful. At one point, we got off the bikes and went down to the beach to take pictures. Jody and I were alone, hopping from rock to rock, amazed at the devastating strength and vast beauty of the Pacific coast. Suddenly I got this bad feeling that something was terribly wrong.

Instinctively I yelled, "Run!" We took off just before a huge wave crashed onto the rocky shoreline as the entire area where we had just been standing vanished completely. It got so deep so quick I couldn't believe my eyes. As we got back on the bikes and were talking about what happened, a police car flew past us. We decided to follow it to see what was going on. We finally caught up to the police car at this tourist spot called Lover's Point. It was a narrow peninsula of rocks jutting into the ocean and a favorite photo spot. The police had roped the area off as a rescue operation was well underway. As the crowd gathered, I stood next to an older man who appeared to be a "local" for sure, and I asked him, "Hey, what's going on?" He pointed at a person bobbing up and down in the swirling water, dangerously being tossed toward the rocks. Rescuers in a boat were attempting to reach this man, but the high waves prevented them from getting close enough to pull him in to shore safely. They didn't want to risk having the boat crash uncontrollably into the jagged and steep rocks on the shore.

Finally, the rescue team reached the man and pulled him into the boat to the applause and cheers of the onlookers. We were all cheering and clapping, except for the older man standing next to me. I asked him, "Why are you not celebrating with us?"

He answered, "Well, I've kept my eye on the girl who went into the water at the same time as he did and I don't see her anymore."

Just then the boat went over a bit farther and pulled the woman's lifeless body from the water. The gut-wrenching scream of horror that came from the drenched man is something I will never forget. We found out later that day the couple had been on their honeymoon and were taking pictures on the rocks—innocently doing exactly what Jody and I had been doing earlier that morning. The older man I had been talking with said to me: "This happens every year here. The people who visit don't understand the raw strength and power of the ocean." I'm almost certain that my instinct and frantic call to "run" when I saw the waves building farther into the ocean saved both our lives.

That was a powerful lesson in the protective nature of marriage. God gave me the supernatural insight I needed to protect Jody. She has told me many times since that she did not see or sense the danger that day, as I did, and she would have been swept out to sea.

Years ago, Jody coined a phrase that we now repeat to each other when a problem arises between us—especially when that problem is the result of someone acting selfishly, which is usually me! I'm like most of my male counterparts. So, she'll simply say this easy-to-remember rhyme to help me get back on track: "We need to choose the WE over the ME."

In our marriage relationships, we need to fight for the "we" over the "me." We need to fight for the knot—choosing to strengthen, not loosen, the marriage bond. I wish she didn't have to say it as often, but there are many internal and external forces that compete against your marriage and family. We need to fight the "me" and go for the "we" at all costs.

Both my wife and I are the youngest of several siblings in our families. We often joke with each other and those we know who are also the youngest of their families. You know what makes us babies in our families? Selfishness. Yup! It's true. We both grew up enjoying special attention as the babes of the tribe. But what is important in a marriage relationship is the fight for "we over me." As I get older, I'm learning that not every hill is worth dying on. Not every argument is worth winning. But "we over me" is worth the fight.

Every time.

We are united in marriage to honor God

Finally, Solomon alludes to the value of a God-centered knot. He wrote: "Three are even better, for a triple-braided cord is not easily broken" (Eccl. 4:12b NLT). Two people, man and woman, bound in the marriage covenant, can form a strong bond. Throw the Lord into that equation and you have a tightly bound cord that is nearly impossible to break.

Solomon didn't say that a threefold cord *can't* be broken, only that it is not quickly or easily broken. If I tie two pieces of rope together in a tight knot, there is strength, but it can loosen. However, what happens when I add a third rope and tie all three into a knot? The strand becomes stronger. What could easily tear or pull apart two ropes cannot unravel a knot of three ropes. That third cord in Solomon's image represents God at the center of the relationship. When we honor God, the knot of our marriage cannot easily break.

Yet too many of us are living apart from each other, trying to succeed on our own without a full submission to God and His Word. When we do, we loosen the marriage knot. God wants to hold it together, but that means we commit to living under His authority and in His Spirit's power. When your marriage knot begins to loosen, or is close to unraveling altogether, the Creator of the universe stands ready and eager to assist you in tightening the knot (Ps. 46:1).

In our marriage conferences, our primary goal is to help couples make choices that honor God and, ultimately, strengthen the bond of their marriages. I believe your marriage is your greatest tool to be a witness for Christ in this world. It is your greatest testimony to bring other people to a knowledge of God, to introduce His power, grace, strength, and love. Why do I feel that way? Because so many people are doing life and marriage without Him and aren't experiencing the fullness of joy that marriage can bring. As your marriage grows stronger in the Lord, you become a beacon of hope for those around you. One writer affirms the advantages of a God-centered marriage when he writes, "Marriage is a major vehicle for the gospel's remaking of your heart from the inside out and your life from the ground up."[1] He goes on to say, "Marriage has the power to set the course of your life. If your marriage is strong, even if all the circumstances in your life around you are filled with trouble and weakness, it won't matter. You are able to move out into the world in strength."[2] And this supernatural strength is something that others will see and desire!

Let me share my heart with you for what I focus on in the rest of the book. Jody and I have been married almost thirty years. This book is about my wife and me making the little, but necessary, everyday choices we've learned from the Scriptures. These seven choices are the foundation for *The Marriage Knot: Seven Choices to Keep Couples Together.* By the way, Jody will offer her perspective at the end of each chapter in a section especially designed for women called "From Jody's Heart." It's a unique and helpful insight from a woman's perspective for both the husband and the wife in applying these eternal and life-giving truths.

I remember the first choice I had to make for my life with Jody. She was living in Connecticut, and I was living in Cleveland. We both wanted to get married. I had to pop the question! I thought about asking her over the phone, which was not a good plan at all! Instead, I chose to be "the romantic type" and fly out for a special visit.

Prior to that trip she was in town, so we got together and went out to dinner with some of our friends from college. They had been married for a year or so. Jody and I had been dating for longer than they had known each other, but we were not married. Our friends cornered us, as many well-meaning married couples do, and pressed in hard, asking, "So when are you two finally going to get married?" Jody immediately sensed my nervousness and wondered how I'd respond as she was probably thinking the same thing. I began to sweat and tried to change the subject so fast that she thought to herself, "This guy is nowhere near ready for marriage. What am I doing investing more time with him?" What she didn't know was I had already designed, purchased, and ordered the ring and was waiting on it to be completed. I was planning to fly out to Connecticut in February and surprise her with a Valentine's Day proposal. I told you I was the romantic type!

That was the first of many choices I have made to display my love and commitment to her. Let's just say it was a little too big of a surprise for Jody, as she didn't really answer me that night—but she said "yes" the next day! I remember her stalling for time, asking me if I had asked her dad. I responded (and regret it to this day), "I'm not marrying your dad, so why would I ask him?" I had some rough edges that needed some sanding. Believe me, now with three beautiful daughters, I've seen the light! I have a new motto I offer to would-be grooms: "Ask the dad so she won't be mad."

In marriage, the choices we make matter.

Before we go any further, I want to share with you an overview of the seven choices of the marriage knot. We'll look at each of these choices in the following seven chapters as we discuss how to strengthen the bond of your marriage.

CHOICE #1: Choose to Grow Spiritually
(Matthew 7:24–27)

The first choice focuses on our mutual commitment to spiritual growth. In Matthew 7, Jesus taught that there are only two ways to build a life—either on the soft, shifting foundation of sand, or on the solid foundation of rock. The sand is a life built according to the world's principles. The foundation of rock represents a life built with Christ at the center. For a solid three-cord marriage that is not easily broken, we must build on the rock. We must each choose to grow spiritually and live our lives according to the principles of the Word of God.

CHOICE #2: Choose to Love Unconditionally
(1 Corinthians 13:4–7)

The second choice is to love unconditionally. Many of us heard 1 Corinthians 13 read at our wedding. It's often referred to as the "love chapter." Love is not all about attraction; love responds with action. Love isn't simply emotions; love is more than a feeling. Love means I'm willing to surrender myself, put the other person first, and put my desires on hold. We must choose to love unconditionally, just as Christ first loved us.

CHOICE #3: Choose to Serve Sacrificially
(Ephesians 5:22–24)

The third choice is to serve sacrificially. In Ephesians 5:22–24, the apostle Paul describes the roles and goals of the husband and wife in a Christ-centered marriage relationship. The Scriptures define who we are to be and what we are to do within the context of a marriage.

CHOICE #4: Choose to Please Regularly
(1 Corinthians 7:4–5)

The fourth choice is to please each other regularly. In this chapter, I'll emphasize the principles of what I call the "blue jays and the yellowjackets" or more commonly known as "the birds and the bees" . . . all from God's perspective. I'll reveal what God's Word teaches about the purpose, the pleasure, and the greatness of sex within the boundaries of the marriage knot.

CHOICE #5: Choose to Persevere Persistently
(James 1:2-5)

The fifth choice is to persevere persistently. James 1 reveals God's purpose for allowing trials into our lives and what should be our proper response to trials. Though many Christians may be familiar with the biblical teaching in James chapter 1, most have not heard it taught within the context of responding to trials in marriage. God has a unique purpose for the pain in our lives. That's what I will emphasize in this chapter. We choose to persist through the trials in our marriages rather than quitting and running from them.

CHOICE #6: Choose to Communicate Respectfully
(Ephesians 4:29)

The sixth choice is to communicate respectfully. The apostle Paul urges Christians in Ephesians 4:29, "Let no corrupting talk come out of your mouths, but only such is good for building up, as fits the occasion, that it may give grace to those who hear." In this chapter, I will introduce some helpful principles that Jody and I have learned over the years and continue to practice today to improve the way we speak to each other so that we communicate respectfully.

CHOICE #7: Choose to Bless Abundantly
(Proverbs 3:27)

The seventh and final choice is to bless each other abundantly. Proverbs 3:27 declares, "Do not withhold good from those to whom it is due, when it is in your power to do it." I love that principle. Not only is it clear, it's so simple to apply. I will explain the reasons we often unknowingly withhold good from our mates, and the power and blessing that comes when we choose to bless abundantly.

Before You Read the Next Chapter

To close this introduction, I want to encourage you to complete a simple homework assignment. Plan to meet three times with your spouse for at least fifteen minutes. When you first get together, read back through these seven choices in this introduction and decide which one each of you feels you need to focus on most. Make it personal. Be patient with each other. Allow the other to make their own decision. This is NOT the time to challenge your mate's decision.

For the second time, talk together and pick a second choice you can work on together. This chat will focus on the "we not the me." Remember?

For the last time, look at the seven choices again and let each other have an opportunity to suggest, "This is the choice you need to pay the most attention to next." Remember: Don't try this at the first time around. Wait until the third get-together. If you're genuinely working on your own areas of weakness and working together on an area of weakness, you can then begin to discuss the other person's area you believe needs the most attention.

Here is one of my favorite Bible verses, especially when it comes to facing the prospect of working on our marriage.

> Clothe yourselves, all of you, with humility toward one another, for "God opposes the proud but gives grace to the humble." (1 Peter 5:5)

By coming with a humble heart to this challenge of strengthening the bond of your marriage, you're allowing access for God to lovingly begin a work in both your hearts. He represents the third strand and desires to play a significant and even all-powerful role in transforming your marriage.

Okay, let's get started. I'm humbled you chose to take this journey with me (and with Jody!). You'll never regret making the choices necessary to tighten the marriage knot, pursue choices that honor the Lord, and show unconditional love to each other.

You're going to do great.

From Jody's Heart . . .

'm so glad you are choosing to invest in your marriage by picking up this book, reading it, and taking the time necessary to apply the trusted principles that God has provided for Ron and me. I wish I could tell you that a great marriage is easy, but that just has not been the case for us. What I can say with joy and confidence is that every struggle, every setback, every heartache that we have overcome together has grown us deeper and deeper in love with each other and the amazing God who is holding us together. Choosing to strengthen your marriage reaps blessings of joy and deep abiding love—real love. So, let's go do this!

Choose to Grow Spiritually
Matthew 7:24-27

*A Christian's real development in spiritual life will always
be revealed by how he or she thinks about God.*

SINCLAIR FERGUSON

The Great Galveston Hurricane is still considered the deadliest hurricane in United States history. This Category 4 storm made landfall on September 8, 1900 and dissipated four weeks later—after it destroyed the then-thriving coastal city of Galveston, Texas, and everything else in its path. Sustained wind speed reached 140 miles per hour. The storm surge was in excess of fifteen feet. More people were killed in this storm than any other natural disaster in the U.S. since then, with an estimated total death count at upward of 12,000 people. The hurricane caused approximately $20 million in damage, which is about $700 million in today's dollars.[1]

Of course, hurricanes are a part of life for those living on the Gulf Coast and other areas vulnerable to such devastation. But all of us can face personal storms that ravage the shores of our lives, too.

It's not a question of if a storm is coming, but when. It's not a question of if the storm will cause damage, but rather how much. It's not about how I will face the problems and pitfalls if they arise, but rather what I will do when they arise.

Storms can seriously fray or even destroy our own marriage knot. How can we be ready for the inevitable crises that will come our way? Jesus says it's about building your life on the rock—so the first choice is to choose to grow spiritually. In this chapter, I want to share five challenges to help you prepare for your own relational hurricane, those potential conflicts that can wreak havoc on the shores of your marriage.

The foundation is in Jesus' words, found in Matthew 7. He emphasizes the importance of building our lives upon the rock. Jesus illustrates this concept with a look at two very different kinds of builders who constructed their homes upon two very different foundations. These foundations determine the outcome each builder experiences when the storm arises. Matthew 7:24 presents the first group of builders:

> "Therefore everyone who hears these words of mine and puts them into practice is like a wise man who built his house on the rock." (NIV)

So, what does it look like to build on a rock? Jesus explains that wise people build their spiritual lives on a solid foundation of His Word. That approach ensures that your life and your marriage relationship can withstand whatever storms come your way. He continues:

> "The rain came down, the streams rose, and the winds blew and beat against that house; yet it did not fall." (Matt. 7:25 NIV)

Then in verses 26–27, we see another person:

> "But everyone who hears these words of mine and does not put them into practice is like a foolish man who built his house on sand. The rain came down, the streams rose, and the winds blew and beat against that house, and it fell with a great crash." (NIV)

The storms Jesus has in mind are the trials of life—those disasters and difficulties we all face.

I remember when we first started our church. We initially gathered each week in a high school in the western suburbs of Chicago. Early one Sunday morning as I was getting ready to leave for church, I received a phone call from my brother-in-law in Toledo, Ohio. He informed me, sadly, that Jody's dad had died suddenly that morning. Her dad had gotten up early as normal and sat in the same spot where he always sat as he read the morning paper with a cup of black coffee and his dog sitting at his side. Not long after he sat down, he took his last breath. He died from oxygen blockage due to COPD.

That was one of the hardest phone conversations I have ever had. When I got off the phone, Jody knew by the look on my face that something terrible had happened. Her eyes welled up with tears and because, coincidentally, my dad had just gotten out of the hospital she tenderly asked me, "Is it your dad?" Then I had to say, "No honey . . . it's yours."

Three of our four parents died during the first two years of starting our church. These unexpected trials and the profound feeling of loss were devastating to us. Had we not had each other and the Lord and His words to lean on, they might have been unbearable.

According to Jesus' story, when we build our lives on the sand of our own wisdom, we risk terrible consequences. Ultimately, total devastation is what's in store for anyone who builds their life, their home, or their marriage on anything but the sure foundation of Christ and His Word.

The Marriage Triangle

This first choice, choosing to grow spiritually, is not easy. Building on the rock means that we build on the foundation of who God is, what He has done for us, and who and what He desires for us. Notice the emphasis is on what He *desires* us to do, not necessarily what we *want*

29

to do. And of course, this is easier said than done. Yet the alternative is much worse. If we don't listen and don't respond to Jesus' Word, the real trouble arrives when the storm begins. How to prepare? Consider the marriage triangle.

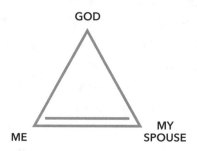

At the church where I serve, we have a concept we call the "Marriage Triangle." We've depicted how it looks to build on the rock in the form of a familiar triangle that is easy to understand. Who is at the top? Of course, it's God. The husband and wife are, respectively, on the right and left sides of the bottom corners of the triangle.

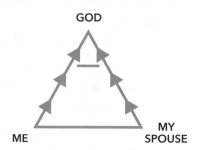

As a husband or wife, the spiritual choices we make determine whether we grow closer to God or move further away from Him. Most of us understand this. However, as a spouse we often miss out on an important additional consequence. If I grow closer to God, and my spouse grows closer to God, moving vertically up the sides of the triangle, we also grow closer to one another as the distance between us gets much smaller. Our relationship deepens over time. The more we each grow in the Lord, the more we grow in our marriage. The result is more dependency on God and a delight in Him. Further, we experience a deepening of our relationship with each other.

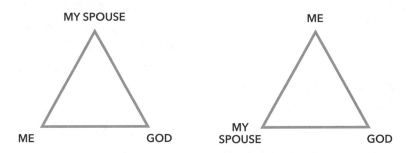

Unfortunately, too often what I see with couples I counsel is that the triangle looks much different. The triangle is literally flipped over on its side. In other words, we can tend to put something or someone else at the top instead of Christ. Many of us put our spouses on the top—and that puts God on the bottom. In other situations, you might put yourself at the top; it also could be your kids, your job, your ministry, or even your marriage itself!

These other priorities are often good things that are given the wrong level of importance. A good thing becomes a bad thing when it crowds out the best thing. The Bible refers to this as idolatry. Idol worship is much more than bowing down to a statue of gold or silver. We commit idolatry when we put anything or anyone besides God at the top of the triangle. Let me offer a simple definition. Idolatry is anything that causes Jesus to become second in your life. Think with me for a moment. That's potentially a lot of stuff. It starts with conscious choices that we often don't even realize are displacing God from His rightful place in our lives. For instance, think of the spouse who becomes consumed with his work, addicted to her personal fitness, or lost in the family business.

> *A good thing becomes a bad thing when it crowds out the best thing.*

As a kid, I used to enjoy watching reruns of a television show called *Lost in Space*. It was one of my favorite shows. One of the "stars" was a robot that was the best friend and protector of the boy named Will, whose family was lost in space, hence the title of the show. There is a remake on Netflix, but it's not as good as the original (although I may be biased). In the show the boy Will would always get himself in trouble and the robot would wave his mechanical arms and shout, "Danger, Will Robinson! Danger!" The robot's mechanical voice is etched in my mind. I think of that voice and phrase in this context because there's a danger when we put something or someone else in first place before our relationship with God. When we do this, we choose to build on the sand. That's our own wisdom, or worldly wisdom from Oprah or Dr. Phil! It's what *we* think is best rather than what God determines is best.

Why wouldn't we build on the rock? The truth is that in our culture, authentic spiritual growth is not popular. What I'm asking you to do in making the choice to grow spiritually is not necessarily trending on social media. I don't want to push the text too far but even in the story Jesus tells, He notes a fifty-fifty chance of success. Some people build on a firm foundation of rock, while many others do not. In fact, I think the chances are much less than 50 percent since in Matthew 7:13, Jesus indicates the right way is the narrow way, saying, "Enter through the narrow gate" (NIV). Why? Because the other gate is wide and that way is easy but leads to destruction.

Those who take the easy way are in the majority. In contrast, the harder way is the narrow gate. But it leads to life (verse 14). Jesus highlights two different directions. There's a big road on one side and there's a tiny little mouse hole over here, and most of the people will never find it because they are taking the easy way. They're building on the sand. Yet they will face destruction when difficulty comes.

Putting it into Practice

I'm thankful for you. I know that if you are reading this book, your desire is to build on the rock of faith in Christ. You have a choice to do that. Maybe you've already been building on the rock, and this is a tune-up for you. Maybe you had been building on the rock, and this is your call to return. Maybe you haven't been building on the rock, and this is the "Danger!" warning to get you started! Maybe your role is to continue to stand on the firm foundation and help a few other people who have been seduced by the easy, popular way—the shifting foundation of sand. Either way, this is a game-changer in your marriage relationship, and it takes a conscious choice on your part to continue to move forward.

God's got a work He wants to do in you, and God's got a work He wants to do in your spouse, God's got a work He wants to do in your marriage. And it all starts with the choices to build on the rock individually and collectively.

If you're one of those dedicated people building your house on the rock, know that you are attempting a challenge that isn't popular. A recent survey reported that only 31 percent of Americans go to church at least once a month.[2] That means more than two-thirds of Americans go less than this or not at all. This trend continues to point downward across our culture. But there is also good news, which surprised me. Maybe you've heard, like I have, that the divorce rate among Christians is the same as among non-Christians. Statistics now have debunked this myth.

> *Only 4 percent of Christian couples pray together on a regular basis. That means that 96 percent don't.*

These results were from a survey where the respondents (who self-identified as "Christian") were asked questions about marriage and divorce, but they were not asked about church attendance. Newer research that takes church attendance into account shows that regular church attendance decreases your chances of divorce anywhere from 25 to 50 percent.[3] Another survey said that couples who are actively building on the rock are 35 percent less likely to get a divorce.[4]

Remember, in the triangle illustration you and your spouse are both moving forward, and both of you agree that He's at the center. Not that forward motion always happens all the time; sometimes we go one step forward and two steps back. But you're both going for that goal of oneness in Christ, and the distance between the two of you is much shorter.

Here's another compelling stat. Only 4 percent of Christian couples pray together on a regular basis.[5] That means that 96 percent don't. In my opinion, this only causes couples to drift apart and loosens the knot. I would suggest that praying is one way of sharing your spiritual growth with each other to keep yourselves aligned as you move up the triangle toward God together. On the other hand, if you don't pray, a lopsided growth takes place where one is much higher than the other, creating a diagonal distance and feeling of discontent.

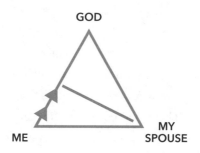

It's important to remember that spiritual growth doesn't happen overnight—it's a long, challenging journey. We live in a culture today where we want everything right now. We want to see results, and we want to see them immediately. If we have a question, we can almost instantly get an answer from Siri or a Google search. We have more information at our fingertips than any other generation before us! And, too often, we expect something similar for our spiritual lives.

We want immediate spiritual transformation, but it doesn't work like that. You need to put in the time at the health club to get yourself physically fit, and getting spiritually fit is no different. It's what theologians refer to as "progressive sanctification." In our spiritual growth, we don't instantly change all at once and become perfect in every way. No, we progressively change and become more and more like Jesus in our character and conduct as we pursue a relationship with Him. To be "sanctified" literally means to be set apart for God's use. It's a process that requires faith, obedience, commitment, and intimate fellowship with Him. The results are the changes that we cannot power up and do on our own, as there is no quick fix. They're often the little things we don't even notice in ourselves as people point them out to us or the big things that redefine who we are and what we are all about. How do you do that? By pursuing a relationship with God, by worshiping Him with His people, by reading the Word and responding in action—building on the rock and not building on sand.

It's interesting that the story of the house built on the rock doesn't say how long it took to build. Did it take three weeks? Did it take three months? Did it take three years? Jesus didn't say. But here's my answer: building a foundation for your marriage on the rock of Christ is a life-long process. It's a choice you make individually and as a couple—to grow spiritually. One writer says, "If a man does not exercise his arm, he develops no biceps muscle; and if a man does not exercise his soul, he acquires no muscle in his soul, no strength of character, no vigor of moral fiber, nor beauty of spiritual growth."[6] So true! So, let me share some clear and important steps everyone must take before this process can begin.

Receive Jesus

Let me cut to the chase: you need to receive Jesus. Jesus is God's Son who died on the cross for your sins. The Bible says that without the shedding of blood, there is no forgiveness of sin. If He had not sacrificed His life, shed His blood, and died on that cross, then guess what? You deserve what He experienced when He took your place. You should have been the one to die on that cross. The problem is, you cannot take care of your own sin when it comes to eternity. You can't make it go away. You can't clean it up and just move on. It's going to come back to haunt you. No amount of sincerity, good works, good deeds, or good living will pay that debt. Only He can because He is the one and only perfect sacrifice that satisfies the demands of God. Here's a helpful grid to explain why we each need to receive Jesus:

The gospel in four words: Jesus took my place.
The gospel in three words: Him for me.
The gospel in two words: substitutionary atonement
The gospel in one word: Jesus

Jesus took my place and yours on the cross. Each one of us needs to come to the reality and the awakening that we must embrace that truth for ourselves. The rock that we've been talking about is the truth that Jesus gave His life for us to demonstrate God's love so that we could love greater. The Scriptures say "he first loved us" (1 John 4:19). John 1:12 adds, "But to all who did receive him [Jesus], who believed in his name, he gave the right to become children of God."

It's interesting what this last verse teaches and what it doesn't teach. In our world, you often hear the saying, "We are all God's children." According to the Bible, that's not true. I don't want to offend anyone here, but the truth is this: We are not all children of God. We're all made in the image of God, but we are not children of God until we each individually receive and believe in Jesus. That's a big difference. That's what this verse is teaching.

So, have you received Him? Do you believe in His name? Have you heard Him, and are you doing what He is saying? That's the question that eternity hinges on for you and me. That's our first step. You may be thinking, "Well, I think I received Jesus, but I don't know how to listen to Him, and I probably don't do what He says." It's okay—we all start out in this way! Receiving Jesus involves belief that is always displayed in action. Hearing His Word, the Bible, and doing what it says. Trusting God instead of trusting oneself. That's building your life on the rock.

Respond to God's Word

In the church I went to as a kid, as the service began, this big old Bible would be brought to the front of the church in a long, formal processional. But it seemed the big old book was more of a relic to be worshiped than a roadmap for living. It may have been just me, but I wasn't connecting the dots as to the relevance of this book in my own individual life. It was read at each service to a great degree, but it took me a long time to understand and figure out that it contained everything I needed for life and godliness. I'm not sure how I missed it for so long, as I didn't understand its significance in everyday living. Just make sure you're not worshiping the book but rather the God the book reveals.

Ronald Reagan said, "Within the covers of the Bible are the answers for all the problems men face."[7] To build your life on the rock means that you must become a doer of the Word and not just a hearer. That's our second step.

The Bible hits the nail on the head and explains why this is so needed, necessary, and often neglected: we must not simply hear and learn the Word, we must put it into practice (James 1:22-25).

Rely on the Holy Spirit

What—or who—we rely on for direction and motivation is also an important aspect of building our marriage on the rock of Christ. So, our third step is to realize we need to rely on the Holy Spirit. We must listen for the Spirit and be directed by the Spirit. Galatians 5:16 teaches: "But I say, walk by the Spirit, and you will not gratify the desires of the flesh."

When we talk about the Holy Spirit, He is the third person of the Trinity; He is God Himself. And the amazing thing about when

The truth is that God has deposited Himself in you by His Holy Spirit to guarantee the results He desires in you.

you receive Jesus is, you receive God Himself. I know that's hard to grasp, but the truth is that God has deposited Himself in you by His Holy Spirit to guarantee the results He desires in you (Eph. 1:14). You can begin to see how profound the impact is on your marriage when both husband and wife rely on the Holy Spirit!

Repent from Sin

There's a fourth step in building on the foundation of Christ. We need to repent from sin.

Repentance means you agree with God that what you're doing is wrong. Sometimes I have a hard time overcoming something I'm doing because I don't always agree with God that it's wrong. Now, I may say it is wrong, but until I desire to change that behavior, I'm not really in agreement with Him. Repentance is like making a U-turn. Or it's like an about-face. When a soldier hears the command "about face!" he does a 180-degree turn and marches in the opposite direction. That's genuine repentance. We turn from evil and pursue the good that God commands.

Relate graciously with one another

Our fifth and final step in building on the foundation of rock is that we relate graciously with one another. We need to make relationships with other people and invest in the people God has placed around us. That means we commit to developing authentic, loving relationships with other people who want to build on the rock too.

There is someone in your sphere of influence who has experienced something like what you are going through and has found a way through by trusting God's Word. Maybe you will find them at church within a marriage ministry or in a small group or Sunday school class. Maybe you share rides to school, or they're at work or part of a team that you serve on. The main thing is, you need other people to help you in making this all-important choice to grow spiritually. You cannot live life on an island—especially the spiritual life. That's a lethal prospect for a Christian marriage. You need God's people for support. God surrounds us with others to encourage us, to grow us, and to help us through the tough storms of life. The Bible teaches this principle:

> And let us consider how to stir up one another to love and good works, not neglecting to meet together, as is the habit of some, but encouraging one another, and all the more as you see the Day drawing near. (Heb. 10:24-25)

Know. Grow. Show.

Spiritual growth is not automatic. These are five steps that we need to practice regularly to build on the rock. We must know Christ, grow in Him and, as we do, we begin to show a life that is transformed by His power. How does this look? Let's return to our triangle illustration for a moment. God is at the top, and you are on the side for the moment. Take a long look at that line between you and God.

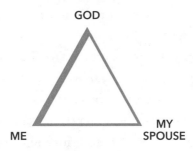

This illustration represents your position and connection with the Lord. Think of it as *positional* grace. What you need to know is that nothing can break that line. In John 10:28 Jesus says, "I give them eternal life, and they will never perish, and no one will snatch them out of my hand."

Once you've received Him, He promises to keep you, secure in His hand. No one can take the Lord from us, and no one can take us away from the Lord. There's also a second way to look at this relationship. Think of it as *relational* grace. We need the grace that is God's unearned, unmerited favor. Why? Sometimes we feel very close to God; other times we feel far from Him.

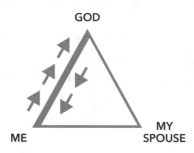

We move up and down on this line God has given us. There's room to grow closer to Him, yet we often move away from Him. Two steps up and one step back. Sound familiar? This is the reality of the Christian life—that we don't always do exactly what He wants when He wants it done. It's a matter of obedience. I like to define obedience as doing what God wants, when God wants it done, with a God-honoring smile. It's what every parent wants from their kids, and it's what God our Father wants from His kids too! But we don't always do what He wants, when He wants it done, with a great attitude. Obedience requires all three.

By the way, we cannot simply transfer our level of spiritual growth to our spouse. However, we can *influence* our spouse in their spiritual growth. We can't change them into the person we want them to be, with the same or greater level of spiritual understanding or abilities or maturity as we possess. My heart breaks for the spouse that attends one of our marriage conferences alone. She wants to grow spiritually, but she can't make her spouse make that same choice. One person wants to grow up the side of the Marriage Triangle, and the other does not.

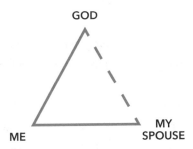

In other situations, both spouses may attend church, but one spouse leads the way spiritually and the other person goes through the motions. One person is choosing to build on the rock when his or her spouse is not. Maybe you're thinking, "Well, I'm in a situation like that or I know somebody who is. What should I do?"

The Bible tells us we can win people over with our works better than we can with our words. I'm talking about you focusing on your relationship with God and you focusing on the growth that He wants to do in you. And that, along with prayer, is the best way to influence the other person. As your spouse begins not only to see Christ's work in you, but also benefits from it, his or her heart will begin to soften toward the Lord. I've seen it happen many times. But the more you talk down to your spouse or attempt to preach, the further you will push him or her away from Christ.

The homecoming queen and the star athlete

Have you made the decision to build your life on the rock? Have you made your decision to build your marriage on the rock? I want you to think about those two questions as I tell you about a couple I know very well.

This man and woman were high school sweethearts. She was the homecoming queen, and he was the star athlete. They went to different colleges and continued dating off and on. After graduating, they got married and moved to the big city to pursue their dreams. Neither one of them came from a Christian home, went to church, or knew what it meant to follow God. They were both climbing up the corporate ladder and things were seemingly going great. The woman was working for a Fortune 500 company and was moving up faster in the corporate world than he was. Her job was her priority. He could feel it but never said anything about it to her.

Along the way, he started making some choices that he knew were not healthy for their marriage relationship. He was putting himself in some situations that would only lead him in the wrong direction. He began reliving his college behaviors and, in his words, "trashed the marriage." He was building on the sand. Though he knew in his heart that what he was doing wasn't right, he couldn't stop the downward spiral. His wife could sense the distance in their relationship and knew something was wrong. She only ever prayed to God when she was in trouble and, for some reason, she prayed, "God, if you will show me what is wrong, I'll do my part to fix it."

Then it happened literally the very next day. She returned home early from a business trip and walked into the apartment to surprise him. Instead, she was the one surprised. She saw a bottle of wine with two wine glasses on the end table. Then she saw something that she should never have had to experience. Her husband was in their bedroom with another woman. She was completely devastated. If you haven't guessed already, the couple I'm describing is Jody and I at the end of our first year of marriage. Let's just say our marriage knot had completely unraveled.

Not long after, we ended up with a pastor in a counselor's office at a local church. Jody was seeking "an okay to get a divorce." I had no place else to turn, as I was immersed with guilt, shame, and embarrassment for who I was and what I had done to the person I loved more than anyone in the world. I'll never forget the loneliness, hopelessness, and regret that I knew my actions caused, as I had just ruined the best thing I had going in my life. I threw it away like it was just some piece of garbage.

The pastor opened with, "Well, I've only got about forty-five or fifty minutes. So, we can talk about how messed up your marriage is, or I can talk to you about God's plan, the forgiveness that is available in Jesus, and the relationship you can have with Him." He was so caring, matter of fact, and directly to the point.

We each considered the options before us and chose the latter. We looked at each other and said, "Okay, give us this Jesus thing." He began to lead us in acknowledging our own sin, confessing it to God, and for the first time, believing that Jesus hung on a cross and died for those very specific sins. Our sins, my sin. Jody thought we were just going to focus on my more obvious sin, but the pastor refused to let her off easy. He was offering both of us the opportunity to receive the fresh start that is only available through Christ, and to begin to build our individual lives on the rock. Later he would describe this counseling meeting—after the hundreds of couples he had previously met with—as the one that stood out to him the most because, he said, "For the first time, I witnessed and had a front-row seat to the act of genuine repentance and transformation of new life happening right before my very eyes."

That was twenty-eight years ago. We found Jesus at the foot of the cross during our struggle. Or maybe it's better said like this: He found us. I have since taught, and believe, that the circumstances of life ripen people to the gospel message. Whether that's through difficulty, disaster, moral failure, even the death of a loved one or possible divorce like us. When we are finally down is when we begin to fervently look up.

We didn't know what would happen to our marriage as we left the pastor's office that night, but we each experienced something we desperately needed: a power washing of the heart and a clean and fresh start. I felt like this huge weight had been lifted from my shoulders and, although I wouldn't have been able to articulate it at the time, I received a new lease on life. We left with the assignment to attend a marriage restoration ministry and to begin getting to know the God who knew us and had just forgiven us of all our sin. We did not realize

> I remember thinking, "I can forgive him, but I don't have to stay married to him, right?"

all the implications and changes that would come because of that first step of faith to trust Jesus' work on the cross. We began building our individual lives and marriage on the solid and secure rock of Jesus and had made Choice #1—to grow spiritually—without even knowing it!

> **Time out!** Have you and your spouse been through a difficult time where you wondered to yourselves, "Are we going to make it"? Go ahead and assess the health of your marriage by taking the Marriage Health Assessment online at **Ronzappia.com/healthassessment**

From Jody's Heart...

Well, there you have it! We were less than a year into our marriage, and the marriage knot was completely unraveled! The question I get asked the most often is, "How did you forgive Ron?" and, "How do you build a marriage when trust is broken?" I did not know much in the Bible, but I knew I needed to forgive. I had come across the verse that said, "If you do not forgive your brother, you will not be forgiven." I needed forgiveness, and I had just received it abundantly, so even though it felt like I was stepping off the edge of a cliff, I chose to do it by faith. I didn't *feel* like doing it. It felt scary and risky, but I knew it was right despite what anyone would say or think. At that point I didn't plan on staying married to Ron, necessarily, but knew that either way I needed, and therefore chose, to forgive. Trust was the bigger barrier for me as to whether the marriage would last.

I can remember thinking, "I can forgive him, but I don't have to stay married to him, right?" More on that later.

What did forgiveness look like practically? It meant a specific start and end to the questions about details. It meant not bringing up past failure, which was painfully difficult daily. Also, I practiced not dwelling on the hurt but instead practiced offering it up to God and asking for healing when needed—and it was needed a lot early on. At times I would ask for reaffirmation from Ron. This meant he would look me in the eye, grab my hands, and affirm his commitment and faithfulness to me verbally, when I was feeling insecure. This he did whenever I needed, though I could tell it made him a little sad, so I was careful to go to God first. He did it with a genuine spirit of love, care, and concern. Husbands, if you are in this place, please slow down. And as much as you want to move on, continually speak words of recommitment and reassurance. It is an act of humility, which goes a long way in rebuilding trust. And the return of trust happens over time.

Maybe your forgiveness issue is an addiction such as pornography, drugs, alcohol, or verbal abuse. Whatever package the pain and hurt is wrapped up in, it's helpful to know that your husband has a trusted and mature male friend who is holding him accountable and asking him the more pointed questions as he's moving forward and progressing by changing his thought patterns, routine, and behavior. Whether that's not going to the same places, not taking the same train, or changing jobs—that's what Ron did! Or, do whatever it takes to make the restoration of the marriage the top priority as you build on the rock together.

Going to a professional Christian counselor or support group at your church is helpful in moving forward as you need a safe place to process and people to pray for you. Listen to me, please. Choosing to forgive is courageous! Know that you are not alone even though it feels like you are. Many, including me, have tread this tried-and-trusted path before you. And although you may not always realize it, if you are pursuing God, He can make all things new. Eventually, even bad memories fade and are replaced by good!

When you're struggling to forgive, just do what I learned to do quite often. Forgiveness requires two big stages: First, there's the initial decision to forgive, which often occurs in crisis and runs contrary to what you want to do. That's done. You can't turn back. But then, more importantly, there are the secondary decisions (plural) to forgive continually as you have already forgiven the person who has hurt you. But now, you've entered the process of forgiveness where you must remind yourself that you've already forgiven them and need to continue to release them. To help with this, I purposely remember all the things from which Christ has forgiven me. Therefore, how can I possibly withhold forgiveness from my husband or anyone else? In other words, I'm so glad Jesus wasn't selective in which sins He forgave. Only He can and will give you the strength and ability to forgive as He forgives!

Choose to Love Unconditionally
1 Corinthians 13:4-7

One word frees us of all the weight and pain of life: that word is love.

SOPHOCLES

When Jody and I got married (you're not going to believe this), we almost set the seventy-five-year-old church on fire. She was bending to light the unity candle with me at her side. To our surprise, her veil brushed the flame and, fortunately, snuffed the candle out after producing a small flame and some very noticeable smoke! I wondered to myself if this was a good sign or a bad sign. My cousin Gary saw it before we did and was about to jump over the pew for a stop-drop-and-roll fire drill. Our marriage almost went up in smoke before it had even started.

When we get married, we stand at an altar, profess our love for each other, and pledge to love each other for life. As I think back on my wedding day, I wish I knew then what I know now. Do you ever feel that way? It's the wave of insight, knowledge, and experience that comes to us through the pain and pleasure of marriage. It's that wisdom we want to dispense to others as we navigate the five-alarm fires of married life.

I can't go back to change the past, but I can learn how to love like Jesus loves from this point forward. And you can too.

More than a Feeling

In 1 Corinthians 13, we find the classic biblical chapter on love. Maybe you had this passage read at your own wedding. Unfortunately, it often has its moment in the sun in the service but is quickly forgotten and relegated to a program note. The apostle Paul's words address choice number two: choose to love each other unconditionally.

Let's face it: love is more than a feeling. Love may start out as a feeling, but it must become much more, as it requires so much more to go the distance.

Here's how Paul describes it:

> If I speak in the tongues of men and of angels, but have not love, I am a noisy gong or a clanging cymbal. And if I have prophetic powers, and understand all mysteries and all knowledge, and if I have all faith, so as to remove mountains, but have not love, I am nothing. If I give away all I have, and if I deliver up my body to be burned, but have not love, I gain nothing.
>
> Love is patient and kind; love does not envy or boast; it is not arrogant or rude. It does not insist on its own way; it is not irritable or resentful; it does not rejoice at wrongdoing, but rejoices with the truth. Love bears all things, believes all things, hopes all things, endures all things. (1 Cor. 13:1–7)

Simply put, relationships thrive on love. Without love, your relationship is like a screeching alarm, a clanging cymbal, a singer that struggles to hit the high note, or an out-of-tune instrument. It always strikes a sour note.

Without love, this Scripture says, "you have nothing." Love supplies everything you need to begin and maintain a healthy, gospel-centered, Christ-honoring relationship all the way to the end. Love is what we need and must bleed to make things succeed. It's the fuel in the engine and the log on the fire. Think of it as the barometer of a healthy marriage. Your relationship is either thriving or surviving, or in need of reviving. And love is what makes all the difference. It's the secret sauce of a healthy and happening marriage. It is the game-changer, as marriages are either blessed or stressed by the increase or decrease in love.

What Kind of Love?

So the question is this: What kind of love does Paul describe? The ancient Greek language that the New Testament was originally written in has four different words for love. Not all of them are mentioned in the New Testament, but they provide a wide spectrum of focus and clarity when compared to our English language, which only has one singular word: "love." If they are not careful, this can put some inexpressive and nonverbal men at a slight disadvantage when communicating to their spouses about the "love" they have for them.

In the same breath I can say to Jody "I love you," and then flippantly turn around and comment on how much I love deep-dish pizza. That can easily leave her wondering if I'm more infatuated with the dough and cheese than my main squeeze. I'm just kidding around, but you get the point.

In the Greek language, the first word for love is *eros*. Eros refers to romantic love. Second, there is *phileo*. This is the word for brotherly love—a strong bond of friendship represents phileo love. Third, there is *storge*. Storge is used to refer to the affection and natural empathy felt by parents for their kids.

The fourth word for love is what Paul uses in 1 Corinthians 13. It's mentioned nine times in this chapter, and this is what we're going after in marriage. It's *agape* love, a self-sacrificing love. That's the kind of love that is the foundation for choice #2—choosing to love unconditionally.

Love is more than a romance. It's all about action. We must make the choice to love unconditionally. That's a love that springs to action when we feel like it, don't feel like it, want to do it, or don't want to do it. We love

> Agape love is "you before me . . . every time."

our mates with no strings attached. That's not an "I'll scratch your back if you scratch mine" kind of love. Agape love is "you before me . . . every time."

Maybe you're thinking, "Ron, I need more help. I need more information and clarification. Can you tell me exactly what it means to love in that way?" Yes, I think I can. There are several characteristics of this love I want to bring to your attention that emerge from the apostle's words in 1 Corinthians 13.

Love is patient

Self-sacrificing unconditional love is accepting and patient. When Paul says love is patient and kind in verse 4, that word "patience" literally means "to be long-tempered." It means "I have the ability to be wronged and not retaliate." Are you patient with your spouse?

I know I have trouble developing this patience muscle on my own. If somebody hurts me or does something against me, my gut reaction is to strike back. That's the opposite of patience, and that's not how this love responds. I'm going to love in such a way that I choose not to retaliate. I commit to being patient with my wife, knowing that God is still working not only in my wife's life but also in my life. That's biblical love. That's agape love.

Aren't you glad that God is patient with you? Think for a moment how long He's been putting up with some of your shortfalls and sin! Wow, that's a fresh perspective that will help you exercise that patience muscle. Let's be patient with our spouse and others, just as God is patient with us!

Love is kind

What does it mean to be kind? Kindness is about extending tenderness and compassion toward each other. It requires full acceptance of the other. It's what we all long for in life—that we would be accepted for who we are, not what others want us to be. Accepted as I am for who I am.

That kind of love is much easier to receive than to extend. The honeymoon ends, and the little crevices begin to look more like big cracks; the big cracks, if you're not careful, can turn into huge canyons.

Ladies, for example, can change their hairstyles. They can change their shoes. They can even change their walk, but they can't change their men. Men, the same is true of your lady. You can't change her into someone you imagine her to be. That's God's work. People walk into relationships thinking they can change the other person. But that's not our role. Certainly, you can do some things and have influence, but only God changes hearts. That's why love is kind.

I sat down for lunch recently with my oldest daughter's boyfriend, who wanted to ask me for her hand in marriage. This was THE meeting, as they had been dating for a few years. I didn't apologize for the list of questions that I had been preparing since the day she was born. My job at that moment was to interrogate her possible future husband. I came early and ready, picking a nice booth in the back of the restaurant where we wouldn't be bothered. I asked him question #5 on my list of ten, which, simply stated, is: "What do you like the most about my daughter, and what do like the least about her?" He was extremely reluctant to answer the second part, but when I assured him I was serious and wouldn't let him off the hook, he hesitantly shared a couple of concerns. After he was done, I asked him if he could live with those concerns for the rest of his life. Often in relationships, the mirage of peace and tranquility finally dissipates when you each learn to accept the other and live with glaring shortcomings. That's called loving acceptance.

Sometimes marriage is about learning to manage the tension rather than completely alleviating it. Why? Because as the Scripture says so clearly: One waters, and the other sows, but only God causes the growth (1 Cor. 3:6). And we must be patient to allow Him to do the work we can never accomplish on our own.

> Sometimes marriage is about learning to manage the tension rather than completely alleviating it.

Love is sincere

Unconditional love is also sincere. That means our marriage relationship is free of envy. So, what does it mean to "envy"? In this sense, the Greek word means "to burn with zeal" or "to burn with anger." It's like a pot on the stove that's boiling over. Our marriage cannot be filled with a simmering anger or undercurrent of frustration toward our spouse. That's what it means to have sincerity to our love. Over time, if we are not proactive, we can allow disappointments, misunderstandings, or unfair expectations to build and fester.

Next, Paul addresses boasting. What does it mean to boast? The Greek word literally means "to swell up." I think of the athlete who twists an ankle, and it balloons so badly they can't put weight on it. That's what happens to our egos when I think of pride. Our egos can become way overinflated when we think too highly of ourselves.

When Jody and I first got married, she had the better job, no question. She was making twice as much money as I was, and she was climbing the corporate ladder at a faster rate. She worked for a Fortune 500 company in advertising and promotion and was twice named Salesperson of the Year! I wouldn't have admitted it back then, but as I look back on it now, that was an extremely difficult time for me. I was envious of her achievements, and my pride and ego were severely wounded by her rapid success. Jody was oblivious to all this, but the Rolex watch she received as top sales performer almost cost us our marriage because of my jealousy.

Thankfully, God was gracious to us. As we learned to love like Jesus, she became more understanding and sensitive to my need for respect and significance. The Lord began to change my heart too. I soon could celebrate her success instead of being envious of it. That was a work of His Spirit. Were it not for God's relentless agape love, who knows how that would have ended?

Interestingly, though, we must also guard against the other extreme—that of thinking too "lowly" of ourselves. In that situation we underestimate God's desire for us and become easy prey for discouragement and possibly depression. Both extremes represent a misunderstanding of God's design for marriage. This is what I mean by an under-inflated ego. It's the idea that I bring nothing to the table: "Oh, I can't do that. I'm no good." Sometimes it reveals a false sense of humility. It's great to not take yourself too seriously, but when you're constantly throwing yourself under the bus, what you may really be doing is fishing for compliments.

Pride: the root

Ultimately, pride is at the root of all these issues. We can be prideful people. The root of the tree of sin is pride, and it produces various types of unhealthy fruit. The apostle James wrote, "What causes quarrels and what causes fights among you? Is it not this, that your passions are at war within you?" (James 4:1).

Pride is what spins us out of control as we desire the world and everyone in it to revolve around us. It's like the guy who's all upset and angry because he's stuck in a traffic jam. Instead of praying for patience, he loses control and begins screaming at other drivers because he thinks his time is more valuable than everyone else's. That's such an irrational response. You can only imagine the damage that kind of uncontrolled anger could have on a young marriage.

Let me illustrate this with something my roommates and I used to do in college when one of us was thinking too highly of ourselves. The non-prideful person would extend their right hand and make a fist. And say, "Check out my right hand, as this clenched fist represents you for sure." Then they would extend their left hand, carefully rotate it around the right hand slowly without stopping, and say something like, "This left hand represents everyone else in the world, including me. It's your world, baby, and I'm just living in it!"

Get the picture? Pride causes you to think and act as if everyone and everything must revolve around you. I'm ashamed to admit it, but Jody doesn't have to say a word when we are having a "discussion" in the kitchen and I'm acting in pride. She simply extends her right fist and rotates her left arm and I get the picture. It's a simple message for me to bring things down a notch or two and get off my high horse.

So how do we rid ourselves of pride? I want to offer you five keys to developing a pride-free marriage. Remember, it begins with you. And the keys involve developing genuine transparency—in other words, learning to be authentic and honest about ourselves.

Five Keys to Growing in Transparency

Our love for each other must be transparent in five key aspects.

Key 1: Be willing to admit you're wrong

The first key to growing in transparency is being willing to admit you're wrong. We have a saying in our home that goes like this: "Sorry is for accidents." What do I mean by that? You say, "I'm sorry" when you spill the milk or drop a favorite glass or forget to empty the dishwasher. But "sorry" is not for sinfulness. Saying "I'm sorry" is not the same as admitting when I am wrong. I need to confess my wrong. Confession is admission. You are owning your sin. It sounds more like, "Honey, it was wrong of me to raise my voice at you. It was wrong of me to use those words. I shouldn't have treated you like that, Babe." Admitting wrong is more than "being sorry." It's about confession of sin and repentance, both to God and to each other.

> Admitting wrong is more than being sorry.

Key 2: Be willing to share your burdens

Not only must we admit our wrongs, we must be willing to share our burdens, insecurities, and fears—those things that keep you up at night. You may not even know what your burdens, insecurities, and fears are, but being willing to share how you are feeling with your spouse fosters a healthy transparency.

Wives tend to be better at this. It's natural for them to share more of their concerns. But men often keep such things locked away inside. Transparency can be a struggle for us guys.

So we need to share. But we also need to listen. Allow me to offer a small bit of advice to the men. Trust me, I've learned a lot in this area.

First, when your wife is sharing her feelings with you, she's not always wanting you to fix the problem. Resist the urge to immediately seek a solution. That's not why she is opening her heart to you. She may not even want you to say anything. Do you know what she's seeking? She's looking for empathy.

Empathy is when you respond to your wife's conversation with these simple phrases: "Oh, yeah, really? No way! How could she do that? Are you kidding me? I can't believe that." That's empathy. You enter into what she is sharing. Husbands, reread those last few sentences. Believe me, you want them locked and loaded for the next time your wife opens up to you. It doesn't count if you try to do this while checking your phone, catching up on email, or watching ESPN. You must give focused attention to show empathy and listen to understand, not to solve.

Key 3: Be willing to embrace your weaknesses

Everybody has weaknesses. Instead of fighting about them, embrace them. Now let me be clear: This isn't an excuse for sinful behavior. But there are some weaknesses that must be acknowledged. We're all different, and we need to embrace those things. Husbands, what's your number one weakness? Wives, what about yours? Do you know your spouse's weaknesses? Embracing your weaknesses brings genuine humility and a valuable transparency to our marriages.

Key 4: Be willing to leverage your strengths

Jody has some unbelievable strengths. In some ways she's a better negotiator than I am. When we buy a car, I usually do the legwork of picking out the make, model, and year, but that's it. Then I send her in to close the deal favorably for us. She's terrific at that. In fact, there are multiple ways in which she is more capable than I am. When she focuses on her strengths and I focus on mine, we are more productive and effective in marriage and ministry. That's what I mean by leveraging your strengths. It helps when we serve in our areas of giftedness and encourage our spouse to do the same.

Key 5: Be willing to celebrate your differences

We are all created differently and come from diverse backgrounds. We each have different perspectives on situations, and God can use those unique aspects to strengthen our marriage. But we must be willing to celebrate those differences.

Jody and I grew up a mile and a half apart. We came from similar hardworking Midwestern families. Yet there are some differences in our upbringing that still impact us today.

I come from an Italian family. In our home life was very loud, obnoxious, and messy! Jody's mom is English and her home life was quiet, orderly, and reserved. The Zappias would have so many relatives over at a family gathering that I would honestly look at some of the people and wonder silently to myself, "I can't be related to that person, can I?"

On the other hand, Jody comes from a much smaller family. In our Italian family, when we'd gather for meals, there was enough food to feed a regiment! In Jody's house up the street, they'd prepare just enough food for each person to eat. In our house it was as hot as a furnace; Jody's house was as cold as an icebox! She'd be trying desperately to open the windows when we were staying at my parents' house, and I was trying desperately to close them at hers. Our family was drama-filled and emotional. Jody's family was calm and predictable. So many of our differences are rooted in our upbringing. But rather than allowing those differences to become points of conflict, we choose to love unconditionally by celebrating our differences.

Love does not insist on its own way

As we look back at 1 Corinthians 13, we've seen that our love needs to be accepting, our love needs to be sincere, and our love needs to be transparent. But choosing to love unconditionally includes another trait: love does not insist on its own way. What does it look like to insist on your own way? It's trying to put your needs ahead of someone else's. Instead, our love needs to be unselfish and sacrificial.

> It helps for each of us to answer the question: For the sake of my marriage relationship, what am I willing to surrender?

It helps for each of us to answer this question: For the sake of my marriage relationship, what am I willing to surrender? What am I willing to give up? If you're a husband and you're thinking, "Well, I can give her the remote every time we're watching TV," it's a start, but that's not enough. I'm talking about time commitments. For instance, that softball league you're committed to on Tuesday nights—for the sake of your marriage is that something you should be doing? Or maybe things are getting busy at home, and you need to be around more. Maybe you're considering a job change or promotion that looks exciting at first, but it's going to mean more travel and less time at home. You'll need to discuss with your spouse to see if it is best.

We must be unselfish in the way we hold the marriage relationship. Maybe it would be easier for men if I said it this way: What are you *not* willing to give up for the strength of your marriage? The things you hold on to can get in the way of the growth and health of your marriage.

Jody and I have spent a lot of time counseling couples ready to give up on their marriages. During the initial session I have with the guy

I ask him, "What are you willing to do to save this marriage? What are you not willing to do?" You'd be surprised at the answers.

Love is forgiving

The end of 1 Corinthians 13:5 tells us that love keeps no records of wrongs. This is very critical for strengthening the marriage knot. Love is forgiving, and forgiveness is the glue that holds the marriage together. It's the sticky factor. If you're having trouble in your relationship, I guarantee you're having trouble with forgiveness. That's what holds it all together. Without a spirit of forgiveness prevailing in the marriage, a spirit of bitterness sets in.

I appreciate this perspective: "Love is not to forgive and forget; love is to remember and forgive." Isn't that helpful? We think we're going to forgive and it's going to go away and we're going to forget. However, the memories persist. That's not the point. Instead, we choose to forgive despite remembering. I understand that my ability to forgive is directly connected to the forgiveness I have received from Christ. I've learned everything I know about forgiveness from my wife Jody as she models it and practices it so freely. I've gained a greater understanding of God's forgiveness as she has extended it to me and others so graciously, willingly, and obediently.

As a Christian, I have a responsibility to forgive other people, especially my spouse. It's not a suggestion, and it's not optional; it's mandatory. I need to forgive, but I don't forgive on my own. I have the Holy Spirit's power to help me.

Let me also add that forgiveness is not an invitation for more hurt. You might be reading this and been in a marriage relationship where you were hurt repeatedly. Forgiveness is not an invitation for more sin; forgiveness is a solicitation for change. Forgiveness doesn't mean that it's okay to get trampled on repeatedly. It doesn't condone sin; it pardons sin. It doesn't excuse the behavior; it exposes the condition of your own heart. Being unforgiving can be like a hot coal in the palm of your hand. The tighter you squeeze, the more it burns.

Love is truthful

This is huge. Our marriages must be based in truth. God's love is also truthful. First Corinthians 13:6 says, "It does not rejoice at wrongdoing." What does it do instead? Love "rejoices with the truth."

Jody and I knew a couple who had kids. When one of their kids was in high school, the wife found some marijuana in the home and talked to her husband about it. They both agreed—after some agonizing conversations—that they must confront their teenager. But their teen flat-out denied everything. The mother was devastated that her teen could look her in the eyes and lie. There was a big blowout, with the parents accusing their teen, and much pain was the sad result. Later, the husband failed an impromptu drug test at work and lost his job. It was the husband's pot all along, and he allowed his wife and teenager to experience pain and fallout because of his lie.

This was a marriage that was not grounded in truth. Unconditional love would have either spoken the truth or at least confessed to the lie—giving an opportunity for forgiveness. That's why we choose to love unconditionally. It fosters an environment for truthfulness, not deception.

Is there anything you're not being truthful about with your spouse? Deceit can lurk like a bandit in the marriage relationship, threatening to steal the life and joy once experienced. Is the Bible the basis of your relationship? What is your truth source? Look back at 1 Corinthians 13:4. Paul writes, "Love does not envy or boast," and he then adds, "It is not arrogant or rude." Again, the idea of arrogance is something that swells up like a sprained ankle or jammed finger. Our arrogance is what gives us this pride that makes our head unable to fit through the door. Rudeness is the opposite of kindness—not caring that our words hurt, that our inconsiderate actions speak louder than our words. Rude words and behaviors are a sure way to loosen the knot. Rudeness leaves the other person with the task of fighting bitterness and hatred. It sucks the joy out of your marriage.

Love is everlasting

1 Corinthians 13:7 declares that "Love bears all things, believes all things, hopes all things, endures all things." When we choose to love unconditionally, we are loving our spouse with an everlasting love. It's supposed to last forever. Unconditional love is the inward love of God that fuels my outward expression to others!

Maybe 1 Corinthians 13 was read at your wedding like it was at mine. At the time, Jody and I could not foresee what would happen in the future. It has been a lifetime of working to choose to love each other sacrificially and unconditionally. But that's what we're called to do. God calls us to live with a love that endures all things. That's the kind of love we choose daily in our marriage. That's the kind of love that tightens the knot.

> **Time out!** Take a moment to pause and assess how you're doing in extending love to your spouse. Take the following Love Quiz in the book or access it online at **Ronzappia.com/lovequiz**

I have seven simple questions for you. Ask the questions of yourself, not of your spouse. Grade yourself from 1–5. Think about the last few weeks as you answer. The options are:

5   Always

4   Usually

3   Sometimes

2   Rarely

1   Never

Question 1: I accept my spouse for who they are and not who I want them to become.

5   Always

4   Usually

3   Sometimes

2   Rarely

1   Never

Question 2: I maintain a sincere and humble attitude when communicating with my spouse.

5   Always

4   Usually

3   Sometimes

2   Rarely

1   Never

Question 3: I model transparency by sharing openly with my spouse about my burdens, my problems, and my fears.

5   Always

4   Usually

3   Sometimes

2   Rarely

1   Never

Question 4: I unselfishly put my spouse's needs ahead of my own.

5   Always

4   Usually

3   Sometimes

2   Rarely

1   Never

Question 5: I forgive my spouse regularly, and I do not keep a record of wrongs.

- 5   Always
- 4   Usually
- 3   Sometimes
- 2   Rarely
- 1   Never

Question 6: I'm truthful with my spouse, and the Bible is my guide.

- 5   Always
- 4   Usually
- 3   Sometimes
- 2   Rarely
- 1   Never

Question 7: I regularly pursue spiritual growth by reading my Bible, praying, and attending church.

- 5   Always
- 4   Usually
- 3   Sometimes
- 2   Rarely
- 1   Never

How did you do? Let me give you the answer key. If your score was:

1–15	Keep moving forward and looking up
16–25	Congratulations, you're doing well, continue pressing on
26–30	Great work! Begin investing yourself in other married couples
31–35	Stop lying! Just kidding—way to go—you nailed it!

Let's be honest, though. No matter how you scored, there is room to grow. Here's the last question for the chapter. Is your love more like a thermometer that takes the temperature in your home, or is your love more like a thermostat that sets the temperature in your house? I'm aiming to be more like a thermostat in my home for sure. Love is about learning. It's about action, not just attraction. We choose to love unconditionally.

From Jody's Heart . . .

This chapter reminds me of a major turning point in the early weeks of our restoration, when we were retying our marriage knot. At a difficult juncture in our marriage, trust became a huge issue for me. How could we possibly have a marriage with zero trust? After what I had been through, why would I ever trust again? That's what I asked the pastor I was meeting with.

Maybe you've had those same questions rattle around in your head. After all, I can guarantee this: we will all experience some serious letdown when it comes to relationships.

The pastor answered me with a question: "That's interesting . . . do you think the Bible says to trust one another?" That didn't sound right to me so I replied, "No?" He responded, "You are right—it does not say to trust one another because we are not trustworthy!" Then he went on to ask, "What does it say to do to one another?" This time I was pretty sure I knew the answer so replied, "To love one another?" Again, he said, "That's right!" and went on to say, "That's what God wants you to focus on: loving Ron, not trusting Ron."

This biblical insight was freeing to me. Though I'm

embarrassed to say that it took me a full two weeks to decide if I could trust God. He was patient with me and once that decision was made, there was no turning back! Choice #2: "To Love Unconditionally" was my new assignment, and these verses in 1 Corinthians 13, which had been read at our wedding, became my guide!

Choose to Serve Sacrificially

Ephesians 5:22-24

Love is all, it gives all and it takes all
SØREN KIERKEGAARD

Think back with me for a moment about all the jobs you've had in your entire lifetime. For me, it all started when I was in eighth grade working as a busboy in an Italian restaurant with my sister, Eileen. She got me the job, and it gave me some extra spending money to impress that cute girl who lived up the street. In my second job, I began working for the Kirtland Road Department. I got this job because I lived next door to the mayor. One of my main responsibilities was to pick up the roadkill in the middle of the street; you know, the carcasses of dead squirrels, raccoons, and other such critters. A very important job to the residents of this small rural town in northeastern Ohio, or at least that's the line my boss used to convince me to do it. That job gave me the spending money I needed to get through college and, if I'm honest, to continue to impress that cute girl who lived up the street, who at this point was my girlfriend.

After graduating from college, I became a cost accountant for a manufacturing company in Cleveland, Ohio, and then moved to take a job as an auditor in downtown Chicago. This job helped me finance the engagement ring for that cute girl who lived up the street, as she finally became my wife. Not long after, I got into sales as an account manager and covered a large territory across the Midwest, which required quite a bit of travel. Then, I left my job in the business world and started seminary at Trinity Evangelical Divinity School in Deerfield, Illinois. While finishing up my master's degree, I began working at a church as a student pastor and ran the youth group for junior and senior high students. I had never even been to a youth group before, and now I was responsible for leading one. God has a sense of humor for sure! Then after graduating, I started a church with that cute girl down the street who had now become a pastor's wife.

So what does all this have to do with marriage?

As I said, I, like you, had a variety of jobs growing up with varying levels of responsibility. And in each one of those jobs, whether it was clearly stated or not, I had expectations to own and fulfill. And the same is true for you, I'm sure. If you fail to execute the expectations that are required of you, then you will probably be dismissed from your position of employment. Clearly understood expectations are extremely important, whether it's with your employer or within your marriage.

Here, then, is a question to consider: What are the expectations, for both husbands and wives, in a God-honoring, gospel-centered marriage? It's a legitimate question that is not always fully thought through before you both say, "I do." At least it wasn't for Jody and me when we got married, and we have seen the same thing in many of the couples we have counseled since. In other words, what are the roles and responsibilities for a husband and wife in the marriage knot? If God were to paint a picture concerning marriage, what would that picture portray?

Each of us comes into the marriage relationship with varying expectations regarding our roles and responsibilities, which are shaped by our past experiences or our future desires. It's really important, as Jody and I have learned, for each spouse to be on the same page as to what these roles and responsibilities are and what they are not. If we are not in agreement, not united, we risk unnecessary letdowns and potential blowups. Ephesians 5 forms the foundation for what I refer to as the biblical expectations for marriage. Of the seven choices that bind us as husband and wife to strengthen the marriage knot, this is choice number three: *Choose to serve sacrificially.*

I think one of the best ways that you can choose to serve sacrificially in marriage is by knowing your biblical roles and responsibilities. Once you know them, you choose to fulfill them regularly and consistently during the changing seasons of marriage. God revealed in His Word some clearly stated expectations and objectives for your marriage. When embraced and obeyed, each will result in much favor and blessing when it is known, understood, and applied.

Love, Respect, and Stepping Forward

The acronym we will use to discuss this concept of sacrificial service is K.I.S.S. What does that mean? Many of you have heard this saying: "Keep It Simple, Stupid." That's my goal. Now, I'm not saying that you're stupid at all, but I surely was when it came to this topic in my marriage. Foolishly, I didn't know what God expected of me when I got married, and as you now know, it led to complete destruction and disaster. Let's look closely at the passage from the apostle Paul in Ephesians 5:

> Wives, submit to your own husbands, as to the Lord. For the husband is the head of the wife even as Christ is the head of the church, his body, and is himself its Savior. Now as the church submits to Christ, so also wives should submit in everything to their husbands.
>
> Husbands, love your wives, as Christ loved the church and gave himself up for her, that he might sanctify her, having cleansed her by the washing of water with the word, so that he might present the church to himself in splendor,

without spot or wrinkle or any such thing, that she might be holy and without blemish. In the same way husbands should love their wives as their own bodies. He who loves his wife loves himself. For no one ever hated his own flesh, but nourishes and cherishes it, just as Christ does the church, because we are members of his body. "Therefore a man shall leave his father and mother and hold fast to his wife, and the two shall become one flesh." This mystery is profound, and I am saying that it refers to Christ and the church. However, let each one of you love his wife as himself, and let the wife see that she respects her husband.

Let's begin with the husband's role. Paul teaches in Ephesians 5 that husbands are called to *lead through love.* That's the phrase that I'm asking God to write on the heart of each husband for his wife. Additionally, the phrase I'm asking God to write on the heart of each wife for her husband is to *honor through respect.*

Each phrase has a theme, which are the bookends of this passage. The first bookend is in verse 25, which addresses the men who are married: "Husbands, love your wives." There's the biblical mandate. Husbands are to *lead through lov*e. The second bookend is in verse 33, which addresses the women who are married: "And let the wife see that she respects her husband." That's her biblical mandate, to *honor through respect.*

Now I don't know about you, but I'm always more apt to do things correctly when I know the "why" behind the "what." So, let's tackle the "why" for husbands and wives. We're going to go back several thousand years to do so, so hold on tight and buckle up as we travel back in time.

This "why" begins at the beginning of the Bible in Genesis 3. It all started with a fruit. I don't know if it was a Red Delicious or McIntosh, but it was enticing for sure as Eve reached up and picked it from the forbidden tree. What did she do next? Well, of course she sank her teeth into it. I can almost hear that familiar sound of a ripe apple being crunched. So, here's my question. Where was Adam? Think about that for a moment. Suddenly, we forget about the husband in this scenario. Did he run out to the store? Was he taking a nap? Out walking the dog? I mean, where the heck was this man, the very first provider and protector, as his wife was dialoguing with a snake? The text says he was standing right next to her, watching this whole thing go down.

Adam took a step back when he should have stepped forward. That's the initial problem. What did Eve do? She took a step forward when she should've taken a step back. That's the secondary problem. She filled the vacuum and the void of her husband because he did nothing when he should have done something. That's the real problem Paul was rectifying in this passage in his letter to the Ephesians centuries later.

> **Husbands tend to "under-engage."**

Today we see the same reactions. Husbands tend to "under-engage." Men have a natural predisposition when it comes to relationships to take a step backward and not forward. You often hear about men having trouble with commitment in a relationship, but that doesn't go far enough. It's not true in every relationship that men find themselves in, like at work or at the club, but it is often true in the marriage relationship. Have you experienced this in your life? Not every time, but some of the time? Husbands, let me remind you of the last time your wife pushed ahead to get the directions, work out the refund, or do battle with your mom or the kids as you stood silent and still. Now, I'm kind of joking, but hopefully you get the picture. When husbands step back relationally, guess who fills the void? The wife immediately turns into Wonder Woman, as is her natural tendency because of the way she is wired. She has no choice but to step forward and save the day. Just watch out for that lasso of truth strapped to her belt. It'll get you every time!

It wasn't that long ago when Jody and I were experiencing a setback in our marriage. It was due to some outside pressures that we didn't have much control over regarding our kids and some changes at work that required more time and energy from me. And if that wasn't enough, throw in some issues with our extended family, which just complicated matters further. All of it led to some deep soul-searching, a few sleepless nights, and a pretty serious call for us to begin to work together on setting things right.

I remember getting up one morning, taking three pieces of paper, and writing down the initial plans to get started on these three problems. I wrote down one issue per page, and I left them on the counter for Jody to see and for us to discuss later. When she returned home, she saw these three papers, not fully developed but outlining an initial plan of attack. She began to cry because she had gotten up early that morning and prayed for me to take the initiative. God heard her prayer. She had been feeling discouraged and overwhelmed as I was disengaged. It was the start of another great season for Team Zappia as we worked together to get things back on track.

I want to encourage you husbands to step up to the plate and "lead with love." I want to exhort you wives, as Paul is saying, to allow enough room and margin for your husband to grab hold of the reins, whether he wants to or not, so that you can focus your efforts to "honor through respect." Remember, he desperately needs your respect and will be fueled by it, though he often doesn't ask for it or know how to "earn" it. So be careful not to get ahead of him, which is easy to do, as we men can be snake watchers at times.

His Significance, Her Security

There's another reason that this teaching is so important. We're laying a foundation so we understand the wholeness of what the Bible teaches about love and respect. I call it the psychological reason. In my experience, men desire significance. We want our lives to matter. We want to be thought of as someone who accomplished or built something, not necessarily for ourselves, but for the good of others. We don't always verbalize it, but as men, we're wired this way. Men seek significance.

Women, on the other hand, seek security and fulfillment. They want to be cared for and loved. They want to be understood and appreciated. They want to be nourished and cherished. They have an overwhelming desire for peace, relational wholeness, and harmony that many men fail to grasp or understand. You may be thinking, "What about the successful woman who's highly able to provide for herself?" We have certainly all met many of these talented ladies. I married one. Does she seek security? Yes. Now, let me elaborate. There are exceptions, but even in these cases, if you dig a little deeper, you will often find that it's still a matter of security. She's saying to herself (for a variety of reasons), "I'm not going to depend on anyone or any man to get me what I need to succeed."

So let me start first with the men and unpack what it looks like daily to love in this way. I've learned this the hard way and still don't get it right much of the time, but allow me to pay some of the "stupid tax" for you so it doesn't cost you anything in your marriage. Then, I'll unpack what it means for the women to respect in this way using a familiar song title from the late, great "Queen of Soul."

How the man leads through love

Men, we must learn to evaluate our love on the biblical principle the apostle Paul lays out in Ephesians 5—sacrificially loving our wives. That's the key to the "how" of leading through love. We will look at five "S" words as we evaluate this amazing, biblical level of love.

Sacrifice: giving our everything

Ephesians 5:25 declares, "Husbands, love your wives, as Christ loved the church." Jesus is our model for sacrificial love. Paul has given us an analogy. What did Jesus do *for the church*? He gave everything *for the church.* All His blood, sweat, and tears. Jesus suffered *for the church.* He didn't hold back, left nothing on the field, He gave His life *for the church.* He was beaten beyond recognition and crucified *for the church.* Jesus gave His all *for the church.*

When I officiate a wedding, with the bride and groom in front of me at the altar, I'll always ask this same question to the groom, "What did Jesus do *for the church*?" Now, I don't prep him beforehand. I'm not trying to trip him up or embarrass him in any way, but I want him to draw this important connection for himself. Usually he will nervously mumble something like, "He died" or "He gave His life" and I will respond, "That's exactly right." Then I will look him in the eye, from my 6'5" vantage point, and begin to inform him that this is how the Bible tells him to love his wife. Just as Jesus gave His everything for the church, we husbands are to give our everything for our wives. That's what true love does. That's our first "S" word. Jesus gave His life as a *sacrifice*, and so must we. Love sacrifices.

Just as Jesus died so that we could have life, something in you must die for your marriage to have new life. That's the biblical definition of love—you before me. It's self-sacrificing.

Sanctify: helping her grow

Let's look at verse 26: "that he might sanctify her, having cleansed her by the washing of water with the word." Paul's talking about Christ and the church. He not only sacrifices, He also sanctifies. How does He do that? He cleanses the church. He gives the church a bath, so to speak. He cleanses it with His Word. That's His truth. Why? Because the truth will set you free.

What does it mean to sanctify? The word literally means *to make holy* or *to be set apart.* That's what our job as the husband is to be. We are to make our wives holy and set them apart. Another way to think of this is that we are called to be a change agent for our wives. Because of their relationship with us, they are to grow closer in their relationship with Christ.

Men, that's a high calling for sure, and I don't always feel confident or competent that I can get it done. Maybe that's how you're feeling too. How are we to do it? Look back at the passage, not with your own insight or agenda, but with the Word of God—life-giving, biblical truth. Helping them to grow in spiritual maturity will accomplish this task. Jesus washes the church with His Word. Likewise, we're to wash our wives and to prepare them for maturity and strengthen them spiritually with His Word. That's our responsibility. We can't neglect our part in the sanctification of our wives. God wants you to be involved substantively in your wife's spiritual growth, to lead her in the ministry of the Word, praying together over the Word, and living in obedience to the Word. Stop sitting on the bench and get in the game!

Some other very practical ways to lead spiritually in the home are to join a small group at your church, do a book study together, lead family devotions, or just spend time reading the Bible together. These simple acts of leading offer your wife insight as to how God is working in you and how she can be praying for you. Stop guilt-tripping yourself for not being the spiritual giant you think you ought to be. Be done with that. Simply commit to do your part in the spiritual growth process and watch God work!

Serve: caring for her in every way

I love the picture in verse 28. It says, "In the same way husbands should love their wives as . . ." What does he say? "Their own bodies." Paul adds, "He who loves his wife loves himself. For no one ever hated his own flesh, but nourishes and cherishes it, just as Christ does the church, because we are members of his body."

When I was living in California, I used to go to the Gold's Gym near Venice Beach. I remember the body builders standing in front of the mirror flexing and posing while I kept my sweatshirt on to cover myself up. They were caring for their bodies in a whole different way. Now, you may not be pumping all that iron and admiring yourself in front of the mirror, but all men, even couch potatoes, listen to their stomach and feed it to nourish themselves. All men try to get enough sleep so that they can function well at their jobs and so on. So, the principle in the passage is this: just as we take care of our bodies physically, we are to care for our wives physically, emotionally, and spiritually. That's the biblical picture of *serving*.

I want to take a moment to talk about my parents, Jim and Helen Zappia. My mom's parents came to America from Croatia while my dad's came from Italy. They grew up on the west side of Cleveland, began dating in their late twenties, and got married not long after. They moved to a suburb on the east side of Cleveland where my dad was working for Lincoln Electric Company as an engineer, and my mom was working for Ohio Bell as a telephone operator. They couldn't have children so they adopted three kids, of which I was the youngest. I look back on my life today believing I was saved twice, once when my parents adopted me as a three-month-old baby and then again when I entered into a genuine relationship with God through Christ.

I remember Jody and I visiting my parents after we had been married for ten years. We sat down with my dad, who was very soft-spoken, quiet, and reserved, and asked him, "What is the secret to a long-lasting marriage like yours?" I'll never forget his answer as he immediately responded with one sentence that went straight to the heart of the matter. He said with a smile, "Make the other person happy."

> My parents out-served each other until the end.

Simple, but not easy, I thought. I watched my parents do this simple-but-not-easy thing their entire lives through every stage and age. From the calm to the crazy, they had each other's backs and made each other happy, always holding hands along the way. They out-served each other until the end. It was like a serving contest my entire life. He would take care of one thing while she would take care of another, no whining or complaining with this old school style of love. Jody's parents lived the same way! My parents were married for forty-nine years until my mom died of cancer, and my last memory of them together is of my dad serving her by chopping up her medicine so she could take it and have some relief in her final days.

From honeymoon, to first home, to the start of the family, to that second career, through the trials of aging parents, to grandkids and retirement, our calling is to sacrifice, sanctify, and serve our wives.

Study: knowing her deeply

For our next "S" word let's look briefly at 1 Peter 3:7: "Likewise, husbands, live with your wives in an understanding way." Hit pause for a moment. What does that mean? That means we're to study our wives. Then Peter continues with these words, "Showing honor to the woman as the weaker vessel." That doesn't mean she's inferior to you in any way. It just means she's different in many ways.

Men and women are not the same. I like to think of it in terms of physical strength for easy understanding. I'm physically stronger than Jody. But that does not mean she is less valuable. You are not better or more important than your wife but rather she is to be treated like a prized, valuable, irreplaceable, fragile, "weaker vessel" of great worth. Treasured! Men, we are made more like a clay pot while she is fine crystal!

Then, look at the next words, "Since they are heirs with you of the grace of life, so that your prayers may not be hindered." Husband, are you a student of your wife? Do you know what she likes and dislikes? Do you know how she reacts in certain stressful situations? What's her favorite color, perfume, or thing to do in her free time? What's her favorite restaurant, dish, or movie? Does she prefer plastic or paper at the grocery store? Do you know her current shoe size? Heads up, it can change—especially after pregnancy. What would she say is her biggest accomplishment, regret, or desire? If you don't take the necessary time to study your wife and know these inward things about her, then there's a pretty serious consequence that's stated at the end of this verse. If you're not willing to invest the time necessary to get to know her like the back of your hand, then you will have a ceiling on your prayer life. If that sounds like a threat, I'm glad I got your attention. I'm not referring to knowing the superficial things about her, but rather knowing the inward thoughts and intentions of her heart—her dreams, desires, fears, and hurts. If you don't get to this level over time, then you will be calling out to God for Him to show Himself strong in your life, and you're going to sense something back like, "Hey, stop talking to Me about what you want and let Me tell you what I want: for you to get to know and better understand the one I entrusted to your spiritual care."

Once married, our wives are the number one human relationship that God has given to us. That means we commit to investing the time to get to know her and make her feel genuinely loved and valued.

Stay: loving her for the long haul

Let's return to Ephesians and address our last "S" word. Verse 31 says, "Therefore a man shall leave his father and mother and hold fast to his wife, and the two shall become one flesh." That's really the equation of marriage; one plus one equals one. It's a miracle, for sure, as the two become one flesh. Verse 32 adds that, "This mystery is profound, and I am saying that it refers to Christ and the church."

Paul is again using this analogy that the relationship between Jesus and the church is a picture of how a husband and wife are to relate to each other. Marriage is quite possibly our number one opportunity to model redemption to a lost world! Remember Adam and Eve? Our marriage and how we live out these biblical roles is our number one witnessing tool to those around us. For your marriage to work, there must be redemption on both sides. Our next "S" is "stay." Love stays.

Men, you have a choice. You can choose to throw in the towel or go another round. You can choose to stay down on the mat or get up. You can choose to give up or give in. You can choose to do the little things that make or break the marriage. It all depends on you.

I remember being at the breaking point when Jody and I were ready to divorce, after only eight months of marriage. I went looking for another place to live as she had every right to throw me out after what I did. I remember standing in this one-bedroom apartment with the realtor, feeling lonely, desperate, and downright dirty as the tears started rolling down my face. I began thinking to myself, "This is what you want? This empty apartment? Is this really where you want to end up? Never seeing or holding Jody again? Was it worth it? You got what you wanted? Go ahead, you fool, and get started on your new life."

> *I began thinking to myself, "Is this what you want? This empty apartment? Never seeing or holding Jody again?"*

Then the realtor looked at me and asked if I was okay. I'll never forget that moment as I think back on what I would have given up, had I signed the lease that day. The joy of knowing Christ, the miracle of a restored marriage, the beauty of a deeper relationship with Jody, the blessing of three lovely daughters. The list goes on and on.

Go ahead, it's your choice. I chose to do whatever I had to do so that I could stay, and I'll never forget or regret it! For me this meant abruptly ending a relationship, changing my job, and recommitting myself to Jody regularly. After a few months we renewed our marriage vows, starting to heal what had been broken.

Now . . . it's the wives' turn.

Wives: called to respect

God calls wives to "honor through respect." Ladies, what does respect look like in your marriage? It's extremely critical for you to have a firm biblical grasp as this will pay dividends in your marriage relationship. Let me share an acronym that will make it easy to remember and apply: R.E.S.P.E.C.T.

R—Revives

Respect revives your man's depleted spirit. Your respect revives his heart, mind, and soul. It puts an extra bounce in his step and a twinkle in his eye. I'm not joking. Don't underestimate your ability to put him on cloud nine as you show him this biblical respect. Paul says, "Let the wife see that she respects her husband." The word "respect" here means to revere. Let me give you three "A" words to accomplish this task. Make the choice to *appreciate, admire, and applaud.* This is what it looks like for your man.

Jody has always been in my corner, especially during the difficult times. I have felt the appreciation, admiration, and applause even when I didn't deserve it. She often reaches back with a specific example about how I have been there for her and our family in the past and plays it forward to get me back on track. She has done this both privately and publicly. To the wife who is saying to herself, "I've lost respect for my husband, and I'm not sure I can get it back," let me go out on a limb and ask, "What is it specifically that has caused you to lose respect for your man so that you would withhold that appreciation, admiration, and applause he so desperately needs?" I know this is difficult for you as something specific is causing you to respond this way. Sometimes you may feel like the person who says of the presidency, "I can certainly respect the office, but not the man!" And that's the cul-de-sac you're stuck living in.

Pray to see your husband the same way God sees you— as a sinner in need of grace.

I'm not trying to minimize your dilemma. However, choose to focus for a moment on the many things he does well, things that earn your respect, instead of focusing on what he is doing to lose it. Fixating on the one thing that drives you crazy can become an idol as that one thing can become your focus instead of God Himself!

Pray to see him the same way God sees you—as a sinner in need of grace. Then, extend that same grace to your husband, and give him the respect that he may not deserve, but desperately needs. Believe me, without those things from my wife Jody, I am only a shell of the man I want to be.

E—Empowers

The next letter is "E" for empower. Respect empowers. You have an ability to empower your marriage beyond what you can possibly imagine. A man's natural tendency in the marriage relationship is to take a step back to consider, and your natural tendency is to step forward to engage. One way you can help overcome this phenomenon is to create an environment that empowers your husband. This will look different for every couple, depending on your gifts and personalities, as some of you ladies may have a strong leader as a husband while others may possess leadership abilities that overshadow your man. Whatever the case, a conscious effort to either pull back or let loose of the reins may be necessary on your part to allow enough of a gap for him to take the lead.

Look with me now at Ephesians 5:22 and remember what we have discussed previously as Paul is rectifying the past problems of Adam and Eve.

He's swinging the pendulum when he writes, "Wives, submit to your own husbands, as to the Lord."

This often-ignored contextual understanding provides the appropriate balance to understand the meaning. God is not saying to become a doormat and defer to your husband like some Stepford wife! Nor does God want you to stop being the person He created you to be.

My wife Jody likes to describe it like this: "When you willingly place yourself under your husband's godly leadership, you're putting yourself under the umbrella of God's protection."

I like that analogy, don't you? While she may not have come up with that herself, she learned it and lives it and God has her back! Nobody wants to be standing in the pouring rain, but too often, she would say, she's counseled women who are experiencing unnecessary downpours.

God has given us a blueprint in His Word to help us live in mutual dependence and submission to each other.

S—Strengthens

Respect strengthens. Proverbs 31:10-31 is an unbelievable passage of Scripture that describes the godly woman who does everything in her power to strengthen her husband, family, and self. She's such a great leader, provider, and helper that she's impacting not only her immediate family but the community she is living in with her time, talents, and treasure. In this passage, she's buying and selling real estate, she's making and selling goods, she's leading and providing for those around her. She's taking advantage of every opportunity that comes across her path for the good of her family and for her husband's reputation. She's not just sitting back eating bonbons, barefoot, and pregnant. No, she's running multiple businesses and organizations like she is the CFO, CEO, and COO! Mark my word, this woman is the complete package. She's like those entrepreneurs on that TV show "Shark Tank," standing in front of the investors, looking for some more capital to make a greater impact. Whether she's working out of the home or in the home, mentoring her children (which is one of the most important, valuable, and fulfilling things she will ever do), she is again working heartily as unto the Lord. Putting their needs ahead of her own.

Proverbs 31:25 describes the woman I look at each day with this truth: "Strength and dignity are her clothing." Wives, make sure you're putting on the right outfit each day to strengthen those whom God has entrusted to you.

P—Prays

Respect prays! Respect prays a lot and aloud! I love Colossians 4:2 where Paul challenges everyone to "Continue steadfastly in prayer, being watchful in it with thanksgiving." Wives, I think this short verse is packed with a serious game-changer for your marriage knot.

God desires that you continue steadfastly in prayer. This means that as you count the many commitments that you have in marriage and life, make sure you mount up your commitment to extended times and seasons of prayer. From the short bursts in the car while you're driving, to the late nights when you go downstairs to the kitchen table with the Bible and journal in hand, be ready to call out for the peace and victory that only your heavenly Father can bring. I've caught Jody doing both on many occasions and it has been a catalyst for my own spiritual growth and the health of our marriage.

> *Prayer unveils the somewhat difficult truth that God wants to change you first.*

Prayer unveils the somewhat difficult truth that God often wants to change *you first*. Whether your husband's "character flaws" are self-inflicted or not, God's way of changing people usually runs contrary to our ways. The answer isn't always in the removal, but in the revival that the trial brings to your own individual heart as His energy and strength see you through. God will teach you new ways of responding.

Be careful, as this kind of awareness in prayer can bring both a fresh perspective and an occasional attitude adjustment. When it comes to specifically praying for your husband, there are some things you can't change that only God can. Those strongholds demand that you call out to God with all your heart, mind, and soul in persistent and passionate prayer.

I think of Jesus' words to His disciples when they were having some trouble driving out a demon, and Jesus looked them directly in the eyes and gave them a celestial jamming they wouldn't soon forget, saying, "This kind does not go out except by *prayer and fasting*" (Matt. 17:21 NKJV, emphasis added). Here's a question to consider, especially if you've been overwhelmed, unhappy, and hopeless. When was the last time you *prayed and fasted* for your marriage relationship to see God do a fresh new work in both you and your spouse? *Prayer and fasting* are the nerves that move the mighty hand of God. Wives, are you praying and fasting for your husband, kids, and family? For that attitude to change, that anxiety to pass, the forgiveness that heals? How exactly are we to do this? To continue to pray passionately and persistently? Good questions, as these are the next two aspects of game-changing prayer.

Wives ought to pray with a certain watchfulness. This isn't just an admonition to make sure you don't fall asleep when you're praying but rather to pray with what I would call expectant eyes. These are eyes of anticipation, believing that God will work whether it's in big or small ways and asking Him for the ability to see it. These are eyes of revelation, knowing that God is sovereign and in control and asking Him to rest in it. These are eyes of initiation as you are willing and ready to do whatever God asks and wants as you seek His face. This is the 20/20 spiritual sight that trusts and believes that God is for you and not against you and that God will never leave you nor forsake you. Expectant eyes in prayer see what others may not see as you trust in God to help you navigate the changing tides of life without drowning—as you watch, anticipate, and expect Him to move. That's praying with watchfulness.

Finally, prayer is a game-changer in your marriage when you pray with thanksgiving. He's proven Himself faithful throughout the Scriptures as He is who He says He is, and He will do what He says He will do. Trusting, believing, and relying on God through prayer is the game-changer that your life, marriage, and family needs and depends on from you!

E—Encourages

Respect encourages your husband. Encouragement is one of the most practical ways to show respect. You, as his wife, represent the most important human relationship he has in his life. Greater than his friends, family, and even his mom! Respect encourages. The Bible says in Romans 12:10, "Outdo one another in showing honor." That's the aim; when you fall short, you're still on target. Encouragement and honor give your husband confidence and assurance. Do you want your husband to thrive instead of just survive? Give him a few words each day about what a good man he is, what a wonderful father he is, what a great job he is doing, and watch what happens.

Wives, don't miss your opportunity to breathe new life in your man by reminding him he's still the one that trips your trigger! Jody often warns other pastors' wives that nobody should be encouraging your husband more than you! No coworker, no well-meaning church attender, no counselee should ever come close. You need to be his #1 encourager!

C—Complements

A wife can revive, empower, strengthen, pray, encourage, and complement her husband with respect. That's what the letter "C" stands for in our acronym. In a marriage relationship, we complement. Not compliment, with an "i" as in flattery—that's the last one we covered in encouragement! Complement, with an "e," as in to complete.

Genesis 2:18 declares, "Then the LORD God said, 'It is not good that the man should be alone; I will make him a helper fit for him.'"

Then verses 21–24 add:

> So the LORD God caused a deep sleep to fall upon the man, and while he slept took one of his ribs and closed up its place with flesh. And the rib that the LORD God had taken from the man he made into a woman and brought her to the man. Then the man said,
>
> > "This at last is bone of my bones
> > and flesh of my flesh;
> > she shall be called Woman,
> > because she was taken out of Man."
>
> Therefore a man shall leave his father and his mother and hold fast to his wife, and they shall become one flesh.

God designed wives to complement their husbands.

Without my wife Jody's influence in my life, I'm left seeing things only in black and white as well as living detached from my deeper feelings. She allows me to see the colors and nuances I need to understand in myself and others.

Now, if you're reading this and are single, you may be asking yourself, "Am I incomplete without a spouse?" The answer is no, as God is the only one who completes us fully. Yet, God designed us to desire significant human interaction. God molds us, shapes us, and grows us through the intimate relationships we have with Him and each other.

T—Transforms

Finally, respect transforms. Remember, God's still working on you too! Ladies, this is the common denominator and summary of this teaching on respect. Just as bleach whitens the load and polish restores the shine, your continual respect and admiration, both privately and publicly, bring out the best in your husband. I believe this because I've experienced it.

God has used Jody and the struggles in our marriage to transform me into the man I am today. I wouldn't understand His grace, forgiveness, mercy, and love without her modeling and extending it to me. I've already said that marriage is a crucible for transformation, and I hope you can say "Amen" to that! Not only does transformation take place within the marriage as two different, selfish people learn to love and respect each other, but the watching world sees God at work and glorifies His name.

Putting it All Together

I remember the first time I heard teaching on God's plan for marriage as I was sitting in an auditorium with over four hundred people at the marriage restoration workshop we had committed to. I felt as if I was the only one in the room, as if the spotlight was on me. I wanted to fulfill these biblical roles and responsibilities, but they had never been clearly shared or taught to me like I had just heard. I totally missed it and didn't get it at all. No excuses and no blame shifting as I was the one responsible. If that's you, let me encourage you with, "You don't know what you don't know." But then challenge you with, "Now you do know, so let's go!"

So, what does it look like practically to *lead through love* and *honor through respect* in the nitty-gritty, day-to-day life? I'm glad you asked. Maybe a quick example will help illustrate. Marriage has different seasons of all different sizes and severity. But, by and large, daily life can be a grind. You wake up in the morning, get ready, one or both of you head off to work, spend most of the day apart, come back home, maybe share a meal, and head off to bed to do it all over again. Throw kids into the mix and it can be easy to let your attention slip from loving and respecting each other to just going through the motions or getting through the day.

Love is a choice; it's intentional and takes work. That's why this book is structured around choices! Husbands, purpose in your heart to truly connect with your wife each day. Take the time to ask, "What are the things that are weighing on you today?" Or make a practice of pausing before one of you heads out the door and pray with your wife. Trust me, simple intentional daily investments like this are a practical way to live out the choice of leading through love.

Wives, how often do you champion your husband in what he's doing to provide for and protect you and your family? Simple phrases such as "thanks so much for everything you do to support and protect this family" can have tremendous impact and communicate your respect for him.

Sometimes seasons change. While marriage is intended to be a balance of leading through love and honoring through respect, what happens when life throws you a curveball you didn't expect? Say one of you has an illness or is in an accident that alters your life? What if one of you loses your job? This is where I'm reminded of Ecclesiastes 4:9-10: "Two are better than one, because they have a good reward for their toil. For if they fall, one will lift up his fellow." Wow, what a picture. Sometimes in marriage you have to go the extra mile in order to lift up your spouse. Just as God designed marriage to be a complement of leading through love and honoring through respect, He also designed it with this safety net in mind, that if one of you falls down, the other can pick him or her back up. And the good news is God provides the strength to do this.

From Jody's Heart . . .

When I think about these roles and the challenge God gives men to *lead through love,* I think that it's helpful for the guys to know that a little goes a long way. Try this out. Set aside ten to fifteen minutes in the evening to ask, "How was your day?" This means _sacrificing_ some screen time on your phone, iPad, or TV. Then, listen to understand. You are _studying_ your wife. Acknowledge that you heard her and show compassion by saying something like, "I can tell you are really (fill in the blank) excited, hurt, worried, struggling, tired," followed up by, "Is there anything I can do to help?" or "Can I pray for you?" Now you've crossed into _serving_ and _sanctifying_ all in one short conversation.

I didn't say "solve" her problems. Rarely does she want or need that from you immediately anyways! But rather to be heard, cared for, understood, and prayed for makes her feel loved—her greatest need.

At every Marriage Knot Conference, women want to

know how to encourage their husbands to take the lead in their home. Ron gave some great insights on how to get the spiritual conversations going. He also mentioned giving them the space to lead, which to me means not doing everything without his input. Try asking your husband a question like, "I value your input, can you help me with this decision?" or "I was thinking of doing this, but first I want to hear what you think" or "Are you okay with me doing this?" Then be ready to take their input and thank them for helping you. When they do take the lead, encourage and thank them. Thanking them for being a hard worker, for being a great dad, for helping you with the dishes or laundry, for picking up the kids, or driving on the road trip. Acknowledging their effort and thanking them for big and little things goes a long way as you strive to *honor through respect*.

Choose to Please Regularly
1 Corinthians 7:1-6

*Happy is the man who finds a true friend, and far happier
is he who finds that true friend in his wife.*

FRANZ SCHUBERT

n Woody Allen's Academy Award–winning romantic comedy *Annie Hall,* there's one scene where a couple is shown split-screen in their respective therapists' offices. They are both asked the same question: "How often do you sleep together?" The man responds dejectedly, "Hardly ever. Three times a week." The woman responds much differently: "Constantly. I'd say three times a week."[1] When it comes to sex, men see it in one way and women see it another! No question about it. What we want to do in this chapter is to take a moment and ask the more important question, "How does *God* see it?"

Why would we ask this? Because He created sex, ordained it, and has a perspective on it. God wants us to have a complete understanding so we can make the most of His gift of sex in this life. Trust me, it's true. So let's make sure we allow Him to have a heart-to-heart with us before we go any further.

How are we to know what God thinks about a topic such as this? Just like any other topic, when we want to hear from God, we must begin by opening God's book, the Bible, and a specific passage that addresses the issue. In this instance, it's helpful to look at 1 Corinthians 7 to understand God's heart on the matter. This chapter will serve as our foundation for the fourth choice: *to please regularly*. Now, just to state the obvious, husbands and wives, I'm not talking about pleasing your spouse by walking the dog, taking out the trash, feeding the baby, or cleaning out the garage. Nope, we're talking about the birds and the bees; or as I like to say, the blue jays and the yellowjackets. This intimate pleasure has to do with the physical/sexual bond designed specifically for marriage. We are headed back to sex education class, with no diagrams, just Almighty God at the chalkboard. Seriously, though, it's all about the intimacy we share as husband and wife and what the Bible says about sex.

There are a lot of ways we can choose to please each other; however, this physical pleasure is one that can only be met biblically within the marriage bond, which is why married couples need to "please" each other regularly. First Corinthians 7:1–6 says:

> Now concerning the matters about which you wrote: "It is good for a man not to have sexual relations with a woman." But because of the temptation to sexual immorality, each man should have his own wife and each woman her own husband. The husband should give to his wife her conjugal rights, and likewise the wife to her husband. For the wife does not have authority over her own body, but the husband does. Likewise the husband does not have authority over his own body, but the wife does. Do not deprive one another, except perhaps by agreement for a limited time, that you may devote yourselves to prayer; but then come together again, so that Satan may not tempt you because of your lack of self-control.

So, which kind of person are you? Are you the kind of person that likes the good news before the bad news or the bad before the good? Because I've got some good news and some bad news to share about the birds and the bees. I like starting with the bad news on most any topic, so let me begin with this.

Bad News: Sex Is an Idol

Sex is a god in our society. Would you agree with me? It was true in the ancient city of Corinth when the apostle Paul wrote this letter, and it is true in our day as well. In verse 1, this letter is answering specific questions that the new Christians in Corinth were asking when it came to the topic of sex. The initial question was the most pressing, as they had just begun living their lives for Christ, and they wanted to know, "Is it okay to have sexual relations with another person?" Paul's short answer is, "Yes, but only in the context of the marriage relationship."

What made this challenging for the first-century Christians was that they were living in a sex-crazed culture. Paul, their leader and example to follow, was celibate. So was he insinuating that they had to now become like him? To make matters worse, Corinth was a thriving metropolis, much like many of our major cities today, and it was full of infidelity. It was very well known for its rampant adultery, prostitution, and homosexuality. In fact, in chapter 5 of this same letter, Paul answers a specific question about a man in the church who was sleeping with his stepmom.

> *Make no mistake, people worshiped sex back then and people worship sex right now.*

Sadly, the Corinthian pattern of decadence continues in our day to our demise. We too live in a society that is consumed with sex. It's all over the place, and it sells. Women are now portrayed in the media as the aggressors and pretty much anything goes. Make no mistake about it, people worshiped sex back then and people worship sex right now.

Statistics tell the sad but true tale:

- 95% of people have had premarital sex; 93% before the age of 30; 50% while they were in high school.[1]

- 57% of men admit to committing infidelity in any relationship that they've had; interestingly, 54% of women say the same thing.[2]

- 20% of men and 13% of women have committed adultery at least once in their marriage.[3]

- 74% of men say they would have an affair if they knew that they wouldn't get caught; 68% of women said the same thing.[4]

We are living in a sex-crazed society. It's true. C. S. Lewis reasons with us in this way,

> If anyone says that sex, in itself, is bad, Christianity contradicts him at once. But, of course, when people say, "Sex is nothing to be ashamed of," they may mean "the state into which the sexual instinct has now got is nothing to be ashamed of."
>
> If they mean that, I think they are wrong. I think it is everything to be ashamed of. There is nothing to be ashamed of in enjoying your food: there would be everything to be ashamed of if half the world made food the main interest of their lives and spent their time looking at pictures of food and dribbling and smacking their lips.[5]

That's certainly an enlightening analogy to describe our current state of affairs. But you need to know: the Bible offers very good news!

Good News: Sex Is a Gift

Sex is a gift of God for marriage. Yippee ki-yay! Or, whatever words you choose to shout. That's the biblical purpose of sex. That's why 1 Corinthians 7:2 says "each man should have his own wife and each woman her own husband." Marriage is between a male and female and therefore sex is to be between a husband and a wife. In the beginning of verse 2, when Paul states that it's because of the temptation of sexual immorality that one is supposed to get married, Paul is not saying that temptation is the only basis for getting married. The Bible offers several reasons why marriage is a virtue.

Seven Purposes for Sex in the Marriage Bond

I want to share seven purposes for sexual intimacy in marriage. Again, just for clarity's sake, the Bible has much to say about this often-misunderstood gift to the marriage relationship. This list is not exhaustive, but is a great place to start.

#1: Protection

Sexual intimacy in the context of marriage provides protection. That's the issue addressed in 1 Corinthians 7:2. The Bible clearly teaches sex is designed for one man and one woman. Additionally, the context for sex between a man and a woman is within marriage. One reason for this design and context is the protection it affords us against the temptation of the sin of sexual immorality.

A word to those who are young and considering marriage: If you know you're with Mr. or Miss Right and you're delaying tying the knot, please consider this advice. If you continue to put yourself in compromising situations that are leading you both into doing things sexually that go against God's standards, if you're sure you're going to end up together, let me ask this: "What's holding you back from making the decision to get married now? What are you waiting for? Is it really that big of a deal or not? Would it be best for you to go ahead and tie the knot and live according to His commands? Or wait longer, but put some more specific boundaries in place so that you don't cross any more lines?" That is what this passage is addressing, so make sure you discuss this openly and make a decision that is best for each of you and honors God exclusively.

#2: Procreation

The second purpose of sex the Bible provides is that married sex is intended for procreation. The early church understood this aspect based on Genesis 1:28, the first commandment given to the first man and woman—"be fruitful and multiply."

Jody and I have three wonderful girls, and although we didn't plan each of our pregnancies, over the course of the first twelve years of marriage, we made decisions and took some precautions regarding how many children we would ultimately have. This was done over time while waiting on God, and with the help of some godly counsel from couples that were a step ahead of us. Remember, our God is a personal God, and He will lead and direct especially when we ask and invite Him to.

#3: Pleasure

There is a third purpose for sex, which is sadly overemphasized in relationships outside biblical marriage. *Pleasure.* Consider Solomon's wise counsel in Proverbs 5:18-19:

> Let your fountain be blessed,
>> and rejoice in the wife of your youth,
>> a lovely deer, a graceful doe.
> Let her breasts fill you at all times with delight;
>> be intoxicated always in her love.

That's in the Bible? Yes, it is. I love this verse, especially since I married my high school sweetheart. This passage is referring to pleasurable sexual intimacy within the bond of marriage—between a man and a woman.

Husbands and wives, let's be thankful for the clarity of God's Word on this topic. God makes clear that sexual intimacy is for our delight. It should not feel like our duty. If you don't believe me, read in your Bible the book of Song of Solomon together with your spouse. That little love letter celebrates the intended joy that comes from sexual intimacy within the bond of marriage between a man and a woman.

#4: Oneness

Sex in marriage is about oneness. Genesis 2:24 says, "Therefore a man shall leave his father and his mother and hold fast to his wife, and they shall become one flesh." Physical unity becomes the miracle of marriage as a man and woman become one. It's referring to the oneness and intimacy we experience physically, emotionally, and spiritually through sex.

Jody and I have talked about the fact that premarital sex is so prevalent and popular in non-marital relationships. Today, people hook up just to hook up, and those who don't want to do that are often looked at like they are missing something. The hard-core truth is that this will cause much unwanted difficulty in your future marriage relationship. We know this firsthand as we had sex before we got married, and we invited many problems into our marriage as a result. We didn't grow up standing on the Bible as our rock and foundation, and certainly experienced the consequences of building on the sand.

Many people have compromised in this area prior to marriage, but I cannot emphasize enough the importance of calling out to God in genuine confession and repentance for each account. Many couples are struggling with sexual intimacy with their spouse because of the unrepented sexual sin of their past. Let me tell you that there is hope for restoration for you. God wants to free you and forgive you so that you can be restored and renewed.

#5: Intimacy

Another interesting verse on this topic is found in Genesis 4:1: "Adam *knew* Eve his wife, and she conceived" (emphasis added).

Now when it says *knew* it's not just talking about knowing her name or favorite movie. In the original language the word means far more than that for sure. Adam and Eve *knew* one another physically, intimately, and sexually. They shared a unity in marriage that husbands and wives are to share together for protection, procreation, pleasure, oneness, and intimacy. I've heard it said that Satan likes a marriage without sex as much as sex without a marriage. Why does the church only condemn the one? Let's expand our understanding as God's desire is for us to experience His glory in our marital relationships even when it comes to sexual intimacy.

In Gary Thomas's book entitled *Sacred Marriage*, he expands our understanding by explaining, "Our God, who is spirit (John 4:24), can be found behind the very physical panting, sweating, and pleasurable entangling of limbs and body parts. He doesn't turn away. He wants us to run into sex, but do so with his presence, priorities, and virtues marking our pursuit. If we experience sex in this way, we will be transformed in the marriage bed every bit as much as we are transformed on our knees in prayer."[6] Not sure if I would express it exactly like that, but his words are certainly worth pondering.

#6: Generosity

First Corinthians 6:19-20 says we are not our own. Sexual intimacy includes sharing or giving our most important possession—our very body—to our spouse. If I engaged in sex outside of marriage, I gave something that belonged to my spouse (future or present) to someone else. God can forgive and restore our past failure(s) in this area, but it does not instantly resolve every repercussion. Consequences remain. We are called to give generously through sexual pleasure *with our spouse* and no one else. It's important for married couples to be generous with each other when it comes to sexual intimacy, as this is an appropriate way to glorify God. Scripture answers the question of how much is enough when it states in 1 Corinthians 7:5, "Do not deprive one another." So, ask each other, in a spirit of generosity, recognizing that you are the only person that can meet this need biblically.

#7: Comfort

The seventh biblical purpose for sex is comfort. In 2 Samuel 12:24, David is found comforting his wife when she was grieving. How did he "comfort" her? By having sex with her. Sometimes in a marriage relationship it is important for one spouse to generously comfort the other in this way. It shows a genuine love, care, and concern that we can only do for each other. We need to be grateful as married couples to God for the gift He has given to us to please each other regularly.

Marriage without Sex

Withholding sexual intimacy within a marriage is not and never should be a unilateral decision by one spouse, according to this verse in Scripture. As a couple is considering this, it's important for you both to seek the Lord together and agree with the outcome.

Many times, this may be necessary for a period because of a past hurt, sexual abuse, abandonment, prior promiscuity, illness, or other physical limitations. These are all legitimate concerns to discuss, address, and not hide. It's critical to be open and honest with each other about your feelings and concerns while exhibiting much love, patience, and understanding. Often, one spouse is suffering more than the other with one or more of these concerns and, if not handled carefully and lovingly, it will result in much distance and misunderstanding.

Jody and I met with a young couple who had not been together sexually for three years or so, and it was a huge weight on their marriage, causing unintended pain. After seeking counsel, they took the needed time to work individually and together to arrive at a healthier place. God blessed them and their marriage because of their obedience to His Word. But be careful if one of you is dealing with abuse from the past. Some spouses have trouble identifying with the type of hurt that results from past abuse. The spouse who hasn't suffered may have a much harder time engaging in an extended period of withholding. Prayer, counsel, communication, and small steps of progress are necessary for ultimate healing and growth. This is where each spouse needs to slow down, accept, and understand the other, displaying the grace and peace that God has extended to each of us.

Jody has done much counseling with women on these difficult areas. I asked her to write down some of the things she has learned along the way. Here are some excerpts that she shares at our marriage conferences.

Often when meeting with a woman in what appears to be a hopeless marriage, where it appears that there is no turning back or no way that any counseling could fix this, she will ask the question, "So, when did the withholding start?" The answers range from two years or more to, "Oh, I stopped that a long time ago!" Reasons will surface like, "If you knew the way he treated me, there's no way that was going to happen!"

The answer to that question tells her how many nails have been pounded into the casket of their struggling marriage. Jody goes on to say, "Extended withholding always results in a feeling of hopelessness. Hopelessness is never from God, only from the enemy, and the withholding of sexual intimacy is what invites the enemy into your struggling marriage. It's not a good plan."

When asked about why women withhold sexual intimacy from their husbands, Jody noted, "It seems to me there are two main reasons women give for withholding: often, it is being used as a tool to manipulate or control, such as rewarding good behavior or punishing bad. Whether we do or do not is directly dependent on the other's actions. Even the excuse that we are 'too tired' implies that, 'maybe if you would help a little bit more around here, I wouldn't have to stay up late and maybe I wouldn't be so tired.' Other times, though not always, there is a pent-up bitterness and resentment, or a feeling of being taken advantage of by the other person."

When asked to address the men specifically, Jody wrote, "Let me give you a little hint here, husbands, to help you out. If you have a bad day with your wife, make things right early in the evening with the words, 'It was wrong of me to ____.' They go a long way with your wife. There's a reason the Bible says, 'Do not let the sun go down on your anger.' It gives the enemy a foothold." To the women, Jody often gives this advice: "Let your guy know early in the evening that your feelings have been hurt, that you're not okay, or that you are overwhelmed and you could use help and support. Give him the chance to help you and get things right early in the evening so that you can go to bed at the same time and without unresolved resentment or anger."

The second reason my wife has given regarding why a woman tends to withhold sexual intimacy is this: "Many instances it's due to some sexual sin or abuse from their own past or present or a husband's struggle with sexual sins like lust, pornography, or adultery." Jody has counseled many by saying, "In these cases, it makes sense that there would be a time of withholding for prayer and for counsel. Current sexual sin or unrepentant past sin, whether yours or your spouse's, needs to be addressed through repentance, abstaining from the sin, and forgiveness. Past abuse needs to be dealt with sensitively and healing sought. Maybe there is freedom from an addiction that needs to be sought and lived out."

Jody goes on to say, "It's important to note that sin and hurt from your past does not make it okay to sin now in your marriage. Withholding sex indefinitely, or as a habit, is a form of sexual sin. We need to help and support each other and seek counsel. Please do not lose hope! You are never without hope in Christ Jesus our Lord. There is nothing from your past that the love and grace of Christ cannot redeem. Hand over your shame and unworthiness to Him. It is no longer yours to carry. In Christ you are a new creation. You are complete in Him. You are whole in Christ, lacking nothing needed for a full, abundant life." Jody wants all women struggling with this to know, "You can have and deserve to have a healthy marriage. You have not been disqualified because of your past sin. Once it has been covered by the blood, the grace, and the forgiveness of Christ, you are free. There is no sin that is too big for Jesus. We are more than overcomers, and there is healing in His wings." That's helpful wisdom from my wife, who has committed herself to the Scriptures as her guide and helped many who have struggled in this area. If you, as a wife, are having trouble, don't go through it alone; come alongside a mature Christian woman for the help and strength you need and deserve to move forward and not backward. Our prayer is for God to show Himself strong in your life as He has shown Himself strong in ours!

Pleasing One Another Sexually: What to Do, What Not to Do

So you and your spouse are to please each other sexually. Great news! But this is a serious, important choice, so we must practice it in a God-honoring way. With love and grace. With patience and understanding. With acceptance and gentleness. With respect and honor. Let's make sure we are all on the same page.

To do this best, I think it may be helpful to address how you are *not* to please your spouse. These are the things to stay away from. First thing is this: ***you are not pleasing your spouse when you're lusting over someone else.*** When husbands take second looks, engage in long stares, flirt with women in the office, look at pornography, visit strip clubs, just to name a few examples, you're obviously not pleasing your wife. I would just say, "Knock it off!" Plain and simple. Get a handle on this stuff, as it has got a handle on you and is destroying your marriage relationship. Every time you do this, you're telling your wife she isn't worthy and you're feeding your head with lust, lies, and lunacy. It's a Dumpster of trash, so stop climbing in and sifting through it! Remember that the woman you're lusting after and drooling over is someone's daughter so you ought to be ashamed of yourself. Pornography is like bait on a hook. It entices and attracts, and then it catches and kills. Among married Christian men, 55 percent look at pornography once a month.[7] Let me say it again: "Knock it off!"

Do whatever you need to do, like installing a program on your computer and other devices to block it, to ensure that you are not exposing yourself to these sinful practices. Maybe you're thinking, "I want to but I can't seem to stop." If that describes you, then you are in a good place. You've acknowledged and admitted the problem which is the first step to healing and ultimate victory. You're not alone. Stop telling yourself that.

The next move for you is to get yourself around another trusted friend and open up about this struggle. He has struggles too, so don't be shy. Next, commit to an aggressive plan of accountability together to help you get free from this addiction. That means regular contact with him to check in to ensure the behavior is changing and an immediate text or phone call for sound advice, encouragement, and prayer in the heat of the moment. The health of your marriage depends on it, your wife deserves it, and you can get free from it with the power of God and a trusted friend.

Next, ***you're not pleasing your spouse when you're asking them to do something they don't want to do.*** Let me share some principles from 1 Corinthians 6:12 concerning the common question, "Is it okay to do this?" Specifically, we are applying this to sexual practices within the marriage. The "this" could be anything you or your spouse is considering, as this verse provides a three-question grid that is applicable to a variety of situations to discern how a person is to proceed according to God's desires. This way I don't have to be that shock-jock pastor and answer every question explicitly that you or your spouse may be wondering about regarding if it's okay as a couple to engage in this.

Again, this will help you *as a couple* to discern if to move forward together is prudent. These are the questions that you and your spouse need to answer for yourselves through open and honest communication. This verse is short and sweet, but it packs a lot of punch as it says in 1 Corinthians 6:12, "'All things are lawful for me,' but not all things are helpful. 'All things are lawful for me,' but I will not be dominated by anything." When you and your spouse are wondering whether you should try some particular practice, the first question to ask yourself is, "Is it lawful?" Or more explicitly, "Is this legal?" Is this breaking the laws of God, which means can I point to a chapter and verse that says I shouldn't be doing this? Or is it breaking a law that has been set up by man under the authority of God, which if violated would be unhelpful and hurtful to myself and others? Or another question to ask along these lines for the Christian is, does this violate my own individual conscience or that of my spouse?

If the answer is "yes, it is lawful, and it doesn't violate my conscience," then the second question to be asked as you proceed is this: "Is it helpful?" Is that an enjoyable thing to you? Is it a helpful thing for your spouse? Is it a helpful thing for both of you together in your marriage relationship? Maybe it's not enjoyable to your spouse. Maybe he or she is uncomfortable with it. These are the things to consider and work through slowly and patiently. If one spouse is hesitating in any way, then it might not be helpful to them or to you. So, this verse is teaching you to stop in your tracks and not to proceed. Don't force the other to see things your way or to do things he or she is uncomfortable with. To the spouse that's having trouble hearing that and pushing the envelope slightly, and saying, "C'mon now, it's not that big of a deal," please slow up and back down.

Give some much-needed space and understanding as you are putting your spouse in a very uncomfortable position. It may not be a big deal for you, but it is a big deal for them, and you need to be extra-sensitive. It is part of living with each other in an understanding way.

Now, if the answer is "yes, it is helpful," and both spouses can agree wholeheartedly, then the third question can be asked as you proceed: "Is it addictive?" That's the last part of verse 12, that "I will not be dominated by anything." Is this something that, if continued regularly in this way, will be enslaving in any way? Is this something that if we continue to engage in it, even though there is no law written against it, it will be desired as the one way or the best way at the expense of everything else? Is it something that one of us will get so infatuated and pleased by, that they will constantly desire it in an unhealthy way? If the answer is "yes" to any of these questions, then you need to think seriously about moving forward as we don't want to be controlled or enslaved by anything as followers of Christ. That's what the apostle Paul is teaching in this verse. This grid of questions is a very helpful resource in many contexts, especially in the marriage relationship as we are called to move forward with mutual understanding, agreement, and acceptance.[8]

A third "unpleasing" behavior is this: ***you're not pleasing your spouse when you're spending extended alone time with a person of the opposite sex.*** I can guarantee it. I know it sounds old school. I know you may be saying you don't have a problem with it. I know you may be convincing yourself that there is no way to get around it in your work context or social life. It's not intended to be directed at the other person, but at you. I've found it helpful to place certain guardrails in my life so that I don't drive over any more cliffs. In ministry, it's probably more commonly accepted to have these types of boundaries than in the outside business world. They are often referred to as the "Billy Graham Rules," and I commend these practices to you for the ongoing strength and health of your marriage as you establish helpful boundaries and guardrails, no matter your work or social context. I personally make it a habit not to go out to meals, or do one-on-one or extended counseling, or put myself in any situations, like riding in a car, alone with a person of the opposite sex. Rather, I seek someone else present or, in that instance where I'm having an impromptu meeting or conversation with a person of the opposite sex, I choose to do it in a very public setting as opposed to a private place. Sometimes this requires some ingenuity, explanation, and creativity if another person is invited in or the meeting is short in my office with an open door, or in an open area where others can freely interrupt.

But again, it's not about the other person, like they are doing something wrong, but rather it's about me and my commitment to my spouse, my family, and the Lord. I choose to not put myself in situations where it could even be misperceived that I would compromise my integrity or have someone say or think something about me that is not true.

> Letting yourself go emotionally, physically, and spiritually is ultimately dishonoring to God and to your spouse.

The Bible puts it this way: "Abstain from all appearance of evil" (1 Thess. 5:22 KJV). This often means that you must go the extra mile, change things up a bit, endure some extra hassle, and make some unique concessions. You might say, "Well, in my job I have to engage one-on-one with people of the opposite sex on a regular basis." That may be true, and I'm not saying to not meet with people. All I'm saying is to be sensitive and understand that spending extended alone time with a person of the opposite sex is not always a help to your marriage relationship. It may put you in an undesirable and compromising position. Or, it may give off the appearance of evil even when it is innocent. Creativity is often required to uphold this principle. And consistency is needed as you may be misunderstood by some. But for me, my marriage is more important than any other earthly relationship.

> **Time out!** Do you want to protect your marriage from unfaithfulness? How susceptible are you to having an affair? Take the "affair-proof your marriage" assessment online at **Ronzappia.com/affairproof**

Lastly: *you're not pleasing your spouse when you stop taking care of yourself physically, emotionally, and spiritually.* For some, a weekend away is overdue, some extra help around the house is required, a change in your schedule is necessary, an adjustment to your diet is needed, some physical activity would be beneficial, or your emotional health needs attention. For others, a major health change might be essential as you blew off your annual physical again. Letting yourself go emotionally, physically, and spiritually is ultimately dishonoring to God and to your spouse. Scripture says in 1 Corinthians 6:19 that our bodies are the temples of the Holy Spirit. So, let's make sure we are giving God and our spouses our best as we work together to care for ourselves in a way that fosters complete wholeness and wellness.

Taking Stock of Your Sex Life

I want to close this part of choice number 4 by taking a moment to rate your sex life. I'm not joking. Here are four emojis I use in our marriage conferences to help make it less intimidating and awkward. We put these big emojis on the screen, and you must pick which one best symbolizes your current love life. It always makes people smile and usually gets a pretty good laugh from the crowd as it makes the point in a gentle and humorous way.

Each of you should choose which one of these emojis most closely resembles your situation currently. Then, talk honestly with your spouse to see which one he or she chose, as you share yours, and close with a time of mutual discussion and prayer as you outline the plan of attack to tighten the marriage knot with choice #4.

Option 1: 🤗 "My sex life is great!"

Option 2: 🙁 "It could be better!"

Option 3: 😢 "It could use some help!"

Option 4: 😳 "I don't want to talk about this at all!"

Reflect on what we've talked about here. Ask yourself, "What is the Lord asking me to consider? How does He want me to respond?" Make it your goal to please one another in your marriage.

From Jody's Heart . . .

In a culture where everything and anything goes, and casual sex is no big deal, precious few enter marriage unscathed. Even most young Christian couples who desire to remain pure often slip up or go too far with each other before marriage. I remember how angry I was when Ron and I sat at the first "counseling" meeting and the pastor got me to admit that I had sex with Ron before marriage. What did this have to do with our messed-up situation? Why was this even being addressed at all? Then the pastor said, "So, basically you told Ron that it was okay to have sex outside of marriage." He said it so directly! At this point I was extremely ticked off. If looks could kill, this pastor was a dead man.

I responded, "I would never say that!" Even this did not stop him from punctuating his first observation with, "Well, you know, your actions speak louder than words . . . " At this point I was *really* ticked and yet at the same time I felt pangs of guilt and shame. I knew that I needed God's forgiveness every bit as much as Ron did for his infidelity.

The truth is that we carry our sexual immorality into our marriage whether we want to admit it or not. First Corinthians 6:18 says, "Flee from sexual immorality. Every other sin a person commits is outside the body, but the sexually immoral person sins against his own body." We give away something that was meant to solidify our marriage. So, what do we do about this since most of us, if we are honest, have screwed up? I love the good news of the gospel! First Corinthians 6:9–11 says, "Do not be deceived: neither the sexually immoral, nor idolaters, nor adulterers, nor men [or women] who practice homosexuality, nor thieves, nor the greedy, nor drunkards, nor revilers, nor swindlers will inherit the kingdom of God. . . . But you were washed, you were sanctified, you were justified in the name of the Lord Jesus Christ and by the Spirit of our God."

Choose to Persevere Persistently
James 1:2-8

Great works are not performed by strength, but by perseverance.

SAMUEL JOHNSON

After that Saturday night, which Jody and I now refer to as "the worst night of our lives," when we were on the brink of divorce, Jody got up the next morning, put on a dress, and left our apartment. She needed help and counsel so she decided to head over to a safe place, the church, which was across the street. We weren't going to church at this point in our lives. I honestly didn't see the need for it. She had asked me about going when we first got married and moved to the Chicagoland area, but I wasn't really open to it. I responded rather foolishly, "What do we need church for?" She replied, "Church would be a great place to meet some people and maybe make some new friends." I regrettably shut it down quickly by saying, "I have enough friends, Jody; maybe when we have kids or something."

Jody waited till the services were over because she didn't want to speak to anyone but the pastor, but what she didn't realize was that the church was now being set up by an Asian congregation to use in the afternoon. After bolstering enough courage to walk through the door, she was greeted by an Asian woman with a heavy accent and contagious smile as she was setting up for the next service. Jody asked where she could get marriage or divorce counseling. Immediately, the tears began to flow from Jody's eyes. This kind and compassionate woman teared up as well.

After Jody shared her heart with this stranger, she shared her own story in broken English, saying, "My husband . . . was a failure too!" Okay guys, let's just admit we all are. Jody actually misunderstood what came next as the kind woman followed up her candid statement with a recommendation for a local church where Jody would be able to get help with her counseling request.

We didn't realize it at the time but that divine encounter with this compassionate, godly woman pointed us in a direction that would change our lives, our marriage, and our eternal destination.

The woman didn't even get the chance to share her name, but she did share something very profound with Jody. She told Jody, "When you go to church, don't go there with *half your* heart, go there with your *whole* heart. Make sure you go with your whole heart." We didn't know it then, but she was referring to a Scripture verse in Jeremiah 29:13 that states, "You will seek me and find me, when you seek me with all your heart."

That was the best advice that she could give as Jody was struggling with what had happened the night before and was pretty sure that she had grounds for divorce.

Well, we did take that woman's advice and drove out to that large church later, not knowing if anyone would be around or what exactly this church could offer, but simply following this wise woman's counsel. When we arrived there it was later in the evening so no services were going, but the doors were open and the lobby felt inviting. I'll never forget the big counter in the huge foyer that so professionally displayed all the ministries that were offered. We had never set foot in a church like this before. We picked up a brochure for a marriage restoration and divorce recovery ministry that just so happened to begin the following night. Coincidence? I think not! But back then we weren't seasoned enough to pick up on the cues of God's divine intervention.

We went back that next evening and this workshop began to change the trajectory of our lives as we learned what we needed to learn, shared what we needed to share, and worked on what we needed to work on during the most difficult and painful period of our lives. This experience is why we started the Marriage Knot Conference.

Finding Hope In Trials

Maybe your marriage trial is not a self-inflicted one like ours was. Not all trials are consequences of bad choices. Many occur because of circumstances that are beyond our control. Whether it's a sudden illness, an ongoing health issue, a problem with your child, a change at work, financial pressure, a natural disaster, or a relational challenge with friends or family, trials are inevitable. They make their way into our lives, sometimes gradually and other times instantaneously when we least expect it or want it. How do we handle the trials and circumstances that this life brings, especially in a way that strengthens our marriage relationship when the mutual tendency is friction, conflict, and division? We handle them by choosing to *persevere persistently*. That's choice #5. James 1 lays a strong foundation for making this critically important choice. James 1:2–8 says:

> Count it all joy, my brothers, when you meet trials of various kinds, for you know that the testing of your faith produces steadfastness. And let steadfastness have its full effect, that you may be perfect and complete, lacking in nothing.
>
> If any of you lacks wisdom, let him ask God, who gives generously to all without reproach, and it will be given him. But let him ask in faith, with no doubting, for the one who doubts is like a wave of the sea that is driven and tossed by the wind. For that person must not suppose that he will receive anything from the Lord; he is a double-minded man, unstable in all his ways.

111

From this compelling passage, several principles emerge that are key to making this important choice.

Key #1: Trials Do Not Have to Make Me Miserable

God allows trials to bring us a joyful maturity, not ongoing misery. James 1:2 says it so counter-culturally, "Count it all joy, my brothers, when you meet trials of various kinds." First things first, the verse does not say "if" trials come but "when" they come. I've previously mentioned that none of us are immune to the pain and difficulty of adversity. It also doesn't say there's only "one" kind of trial but "various" kinds of trials. So, it's not a one size fits all when it comes to the pain and problems we face. We don't pick our trials. They seem to pick on us, and they aren't the same for each individual as we all wrestle with various degrees and forms of crises. It's interesting to note that the original context of this letter addresses the difficulty that often comes when sharing your faith in a hostile world. This is what these early Christians were facing. But the principles that James states can be applied to various kinds of life's setbacks. The text commands us to "count it all joy."

> Avoidance and denial put up a wall that blocks people from coming to your aid.

Now please understand that neither I nor James in this passage is saying to go ahead and paint a fake smile on your face and act like everything is okay when it's not. Pretending like all is well when you are burdened or suffering only leads to more avoidance and denial. Avoidance and denial in effect put up a wall. That wall blocks people from being able to come to your aid and offer compassion and encouragement.

Imagine if Jody had put up a wall of defense instead of going to the church across the street that day and opening up her heart to that caring and helpful woman. Where would we both be now? I don't even want to know!

What I do know is that God wanted us to learn something then so we could help people now. History has a way of repeating itself and hunting you down when you refuse to humble yourself and grow. Let me sum it up like this: Trials are God-given opportunities for each of us to seek help, support, and counsel from others, and most importantly from God. And such hard times don't have to make us miserable.

Key #2: Trials Test My Faith

God allows trials in our marriage to strengthen our faith.

Verse 3 states, "for you know . . ." We are aware of something that not everyone knows, believes, or grasps. Everything you're going through in this life that is causing you headache, heartache, and harm—from that little argument in your marriage that blows up into the big meltdown to that flat tire on your way to work that made you so late—they are all there to test your faith. That's what we as Christians are supposed to know to understand trials, endure them, and sometimes overcome them. The result is a deeper trust in the Lord.

That's what James is talking about when he says, "The testing of your faith produces steadfastness" (James 1:3). Your trial is a test. Here's a question to consider before we move forward: When you were a kid in school, did you like taking tests? Some people would say yes (you valedictorians know who you are), while others of us would say no, as we didn't like the pressure and anxiety that tests brought, whether we were prepared or not.

In the same way, God doesn't grade us according to the normal grading scale. We aren't given an A, B, C, D, or F depending on how we respond to the trial. God grades on a curve. He's more interested in the experience and our response and the way in which it draws us closer to Him.

I remember several instances when this became extremely clear to me. One of them was when Jody and I were expecting a third child. We were so surprised, excited, and thankful. And then came a

> **We had to decide if we trusted God, the Giver of this little life, when He chose to take it back.**

pain-stricken evening while we were out with some friends. Jody looked at me and I knew immediately that something was terribly wrong. Next thing you know, we were making an excuse to leave early and driving straight to the nearest hospital as Jody was suffering a miscarriage. The sudden loss of life and the joy it was promising could have either caused us to run away from God with blame, anger, and resentment, or run to Him with all our despair, questions, and discouragement. We had to decide if we trusted God, the Giver of this little life, when He chose to take it back. Over time we realized He was wanting us to trust Him on a much deeper level. He taught us to comfort other types of couples who face this type of loss. We became a little more like Jesus through that heartbreaking period. We are grateful for how God has tested our faith.

Key #3: Tests of Faith Produce Endurance

God has a purpose in your pain, even if it has to do with your marriage. His desire is to funnel down deep inside of you something that only comes because of adversity and difficulty. He can't get it to you through any other means or any other way. Tests of faith produce endurance. That's the characteristic that God wants to see fully downloaded, developed, and displayed in you. James describes a test that results in a deeper steadfastness (verse 3).

The word *steadfastness* comes from a compound word in the original language that the New Testament was written in. Let me break that compound word down for you so that we have complete understanding. The first part literally means "under" and the second part means "to remain." So, when you put them both together, it's a command and call "to remain under." To withstand the pressure. To not cut and run. Imagine yourself sitting down in a chair, with all 6'5" of me standing behind you, placing my hands upon your shoulders. Then I put my full weight, which is approximately 250 pounds, pressing down upon you. Your first reaction is not likely to stay under it and ask for more of it. No, of course not. Your natural reaction is to get out from under it or squirm away from it. That's the picture of this compound word translated "steadfastness" or "perseverance" or "endurance."

Endurance is that quality of faith that God desires to form in us through adversity. He wants us to remain under life's weight to produce something in us that we can't produce in ourselves. But too often when the weight of this world is upon our shoulders we want to squirm away and cut loose. What we are talking about is something I refer to as staying power. It's developed during the trials of life as our faith is tested beyond our human limitations. That's what God is desiring to curate and cultivate in you through adversity and difficulty. Let me say it again: life's pain is meant to result in God's gain.

The perfect example of this staying power is found in Genesis chapters 37 through 50. It's the story of Joseph. Joseph had nowhere to run. He was unfairly treated by his brothers by being thrown into a pit and left to die and then falsely accused of trying to rape the wife of a dignitary. Joseph ends up in jail for three years though totally innocent. He patiently waited for God's purpose to be fulfilled. Years later, after Joseph found favor with the king of that land, God used him to bring about His ordained purposes. His brothers became his subjects and were humbled under his newly found significance. Trembling now in fear of his power to retaliate, Joseph makes a remarkable statement that sets everything straight: "As for you, you meant evil against me, but God meant it for good" (Gen. 50:20).

Despite the surroundings, Joseph bloomed where he was planted. He understood how trials produced God's perfect purposes. We can embrace that principle too. Whether it's that unfair situation at work, that seemingly unresolvable problem at home, or that long line at the DMV, each can test our patience to the limit! God wants to use all this life's uncertainty to produce endurance, or staying power in His children. The same is true for hard times in our marriages.

Key #4: Endurance Develops Godly Character

God wants to manage your period of trial in such a way that He uses it to develop and grow your character. James 1:4 states,

> And let steadfastness have its full effect, that you may be perfect and complete, lacking in nothing.

That's a picture of Christian maturity, wholeness, and wellness. When James refers to "perfect and complete," he's not implying that you're never going to have a problem and that life will always feel fair. Rather, it's through the process of learning to endure such hard times that He forms a Christlike character in you. A trial is a circumstance allowed by God to help you look to God, lean on God, and learn from God. It helps you to take a personal inventory of yourself as you look up for divine intervention and look within for spiritual transformation. When we face problems, God's desire is that we would embrace trials exclusively and exhaustively to become a better version of ourselves and to become more like Christ.

I recall a period when Jody and I went through a challenging season with one of our girls that lasted over a year. It was a difficult time for me as a parent because I was watching from the sideline, so to speak, as a person in authority in my daughter's life was treating her unjustly and tearing her down in front of others. There was nothing I could do to fix the situation. I had to watch her endure. She was working so hard, proving herself over and over. As time went on, that person never made it right by building her back up. It left our sweet daughter feeling inadequate and insecure. I was counseled by some experts in this field to not take matters into my own hands, but instead to work behind the scenes to coach my daughter on how to resolve this herself. She was now at an age that warranted that kind of parenting switch, and she would most likely learn more from working through it on her own. I confess, I did not resist the temptation to get involved. I didn't handle it very well. Yet God, in His gracious goodness, still used this trial in the life of my daughter to grow and mature her in her faith. She developed a remarkable level of maturity and godly character and womanhood as she endured this difficulty with such grace, humility, and perseverance. God used this nasty experience to forge many godly characteristics into my daughter that I see revealed in her today.

That's how trials can test your faith too. And tests of faith are supposed to produce something in each of us as followers of Christ that we can't produce on our own. That's endurance. And endurance gives us godly character as we lean into God and learn from Him as the fire gets hotter and hotter. He uses the difficulty we experience in marriage to define and refine us into the couple that can reflect His attributes and glory so others can be drawn closer to Him. Your marriage relationship is a crucible for godly growth, maturity, and the building up of godly character. And godly character requires something more.

> We would all say we want spiritual wisdom, but there is only one clear path for getting it.

Key #5: Godly Character Requires Spiritual Wisdom

The fifth key is that godly character requires spiritual wisdom. I think we would all say we want spiritual wisdom, but there is only one clear path to getting it, especially when amid trouble and trials. James 1:5 makes it clear:

> If any of you lacks wisdom, let him ask God, who gives generously to all without reproach, and it will be given him.

Wisdom comes from asking God. This of course is prayer. It means bringing your need for wisdom to your Creator and Sustainer. Your heavenly Father who loves you, cares for you, and wants to hear from you also desires to grant you wisdom generously.

If you want to hear from God, let me save you some time and tell you the primary ways He speaks to His people. First and foremost, God speaks through His Word, the Bible. This is the primary vehicle He uses. That's why we've been sharing so much Scripture in each of these choices to keep couples strengthened together. God wants to give guidance and His guidance comes directly from His Word. Secondly, God communicates to His people from a person who is speaking through His Word. Again, that's what I'm trying to accomplish as I share some very meaningful Scriptures that God has used in Jody's and my life. This can also come through a friend, a pastor, or another book or sermon. Proverbs 11:14 reminds us of how important this is when it says, "Where there is no guidance, a people falls, but in an abundance of counselors there is safety." Thirdly, God speaks through other people who are not referencing the Bible when they have a fresh insight or encouragement for you that doesn't contradict what the Bible teaches. Worship songs, radio pastors, podcasts have often been used to answer a question I'm struggling with or calm my anxious heart as well as a random encounter with a stranger who brings a word of encouragement or wisdom.

God wants to hear from you so that He can dish out spiritual wisdom. He's ready and willing.

My mom was a great cook, and she used to tell us the stories of how our relatives would swap recipes with each other. She told us about one of my aunts, who will remain nameless, who would willingly share a recipe when asked but would knowingly leave out a key ingredient so that when someone else made it, it would not taste the same. Seriously, we all laughed at this, and I certainly don't want to start a family feud, but God isn't like that aunt of mine! He never leaves out any key ingredients as He's always ready and willing to give you the wisdom, strength, guidance, and counsel you need. He may not give you all you want at once, but He certainly will give you all you need for the moment. Sometimes that's an increased sense of His presence, a divine insight or some much needed sacred strength which will help you in your time of need. The text says that He gives "generously . . . without reproach." That means He's not holding back, not making you beg, and not playing some game with you. God's desire for His children during periods of adversity is that we would call out to Him! I love the verse in Jeremiah 33:3 that says, "Call to me and I will answer you, and will tell you great and hidden things."

Spiritual wisdom is not a matter of education; spiritual wisdom is a matter of prayer. And believe me when I tell you, you're one conversation away!

James 1:6 offers another important principle: "But let him *ask in faith, with no doubting*, for the one who doubts is like a wave of the sea that is driven and tossed by the wind" (emphasis added).

This verse is making a distinction between the husband or wife, man or woman, who is going to God to *bargain* with Him instead of *trusting* in Him. To *gamble* with Him instead of *depending* on Him. To *ask* something of Him instead of wanting to *know* Him. Or to prove himself to Him instead of believing in Him. That's not the best way to go about it at all. In fact, James warns, "For that person must not suppose that he will receive anything from the Lord; he is a double-minded man, unstable in all his ways" (verses 7–8).

Remember the scene in the classic movie *It's a Wonderful Life* where Jimmy Stewart is playing George Bailey? He's at the bar with a drink in his hand and he begins to pray, "God . . . God . . . Dear Father in heaven, I'm not a praying man, but if you're up there and if you can hear me, show me the way. I'm at the end of my rope. Show me the way." Then after George takes a punch, Clarence, the inexperienced guardian angel that was assigned to him to earn his wings, shows up to point him in the right direction. I'm not saying that was a bad prayer as it certainly seemed humble, and God did respond Hollywood-style. But it borders and teeters on unbelief and an uncertainty of God's existence and responsiveness.

Let's believe God when we call to Him in prayer. Let's lean confidently on the rock, truly believing in Jesus, and trusting in His Word.

Key #6: Spiritual Wisdom Is a Reward from God

Notice the blessing that comes to the person or couple that stays under the difficulty to learn the lesson that God wants to teach. If you go down further in the chapter, James 1:12 says, "Blessed is the man who remains steadfast under trial, for when he has stood the test he will receive the crown of life, which God has promised to those who love him."

That's a wonderful and amazing picture. When we remain steadfast in our faith in this life, we will certainly be rewarded in the next. There aren't many guarantees in this life, I'll tell you that. But this promise is worth betting it all on. In the text it's referring to that ultimate eternal reward which we will experience in heaven. Seeing God, face-to-face, saying, "Well done, good and faithful servant." But there are also rewards in this life. When you stand the test of time and persevere persistently, you experience the closeness of God, the intimacy of His presence, and an experience of His miraculous power.

I don't know where I would be without the confidence and assurance that comes from walking in His path and promises. The peace that surpasses all understanding as you rest in His provision and power.

I remember when our youngest daughter, Emily, broke her femur. We never got all the details to this story, and I don't think we ever will as they may have sworn themselves to secrecy, but all three of our girls were horsing around in the basement when I got home from work. Four or five steps up to the second floor bedroom, and I heard the loudest scream that ever came out of one of our girls before! I ran downstairs, grabbed Emily in my arms, put her in the car, and rushed her to the hospital. When we returned that night she was in a wheelchair with a body cast that extended from her chest to ankle as the largest bone in her little body had been snapped in half.

As she fell asleep, the first night in the wheelchair in the family room,

I lay down on the couch to sleep next to her, as I didn't want her to be alone. Before falling asleep, I replayed every second of the incident in my mind. "Why didn't I just go downstairs first as I would have headed this whole thing off?" I thought to myself. And: "How foolish of me that I just didn't go directly downstairs to check on all three of them." At about 2:15 a.m. Emily woke me up by saying, "Dad, Dad, are you awake?" My groggy response, "Yep, Em, I am now." She replied, "Dad, I can move my arms." And I said, "Good, Em." Then thirty seconds later she replied. "Dad, I can move my other leg." I responded, "Good, Em." Then another minute went by and she said, "Dad, are you awake? Because I can move my toes." And I said "Good, Em." Then another few minutes went by and she said, "Dad, I can move my head." And I responded, "Yep, Em, and you can move your mouth too so just go back to sleep."

After we laughed it off, and she started to doze again I thought to myself, this kindergartener of mine, instead of complaining and whining, is joyfully counting her blessings. What a humbling lesson I learned that night. Let's all learn from my little one as we make the choice to persevere persistently. First Thessalonians 5:17–18 says it all, so go ahead and post it on your wall: "Pray without ceasing, give thanks in all circumstances; for this is the will of God in Christ Jesus for you."

During the Marriage Knot Conferences, we typically close our discussion of Choice # 5 by going into a time of prayer. We recognize that many couples are wrestling with many things, and this session can be extremely difficult as people are carrying heavy burdens that are finally revealed and acknowledged. I'll ask the couples to pray through this passage of Scripture in James 1 together as they ask God for help, healing, and hope. Often, I open my Bible and read from Psalm 34—a psalm I commend to you too, no matter the trial you face. As a side note, I've found it extremely helpful to pray the Scriptures back to God, especially when I'm struggling with what and how to pray. It has become a regular part of my spiritual disciplines, I've taught our church family to do it, and I encourage you to do the same.

From Jody's Heart . . .

Let's be honest! When faced with unexpected bad news or struggling in a difficult marriage or suffering from loss, be it health, job, or a broken relationship, our first response is usually anything but joyful. Is it just me or have you ever wondered, "God, why?" "Why this, why me, why now?" or "God, are You kidding me?" Somewhere along the way I feel like I was taught not to ask God "why" questions. I get it that some would say the "better" questions might be, "What do You want me to do?" or, considering the teaching here in James 1, maybe, "What do You want to teach me?" or "How do You want to change me?" and so on. I do not disagree with asking those great questions, and yet I have not found evidence in people's encounters with Jesus that would say He had a problem with His friends and associates asking Him the honest question on their heart: "Why?"

Especially they would ask this when they were confused or despairing. For instance, in John 9:1–3 His disciples were asking Jesus why the man had been born blind. Jesus wasn't offended. He corrected the false teaching of the day and then answered the question. "It was not that this man sinned, or his parents, but that the works of God might be displayed in him." Wow! Don't we sometimes feel "cursed" in the middle of hard times? When instead, quite possibly, God has chosen us to display His works in or through us through this suffering.

The first thing that Mary and Martha both said to Jesus, after Lazarus had died, was "Lord, if you had been here . . . " I'm thinking that maybe they too had been taught not to ask God, "Why?" because I think at the root of their state-ment is the question, "Lord, why didn't you come sooner when we called for You? Why did You not come immedi-ately?" Most heartbreaking, "Why did You let Your friend, our brother, die?"

Again, Jesus wasn't put off or offended. He understood and answered Martha plainly that her brother would rise and that whoever believes in Him would never die—His resurrection power was about to be displayed. With Mary, He wasn't angry that she questioned. He understood where she was coming from and her confusion. He felt her pain, entered the sorrow she was feeling, and utterly wept with her. Jesus is not above weeping with you! He will meet you too: with His promise never to leave you. Perseverance isn't easy! Jesus understands! In Mark 15:34, on the cross, suffering unimaginable pain, on the verge of death, Jesus asked, "My God, My God, why have you forsaken me?" Then what did He do? He willingly gave His Father His spirit—His very life.

I love how James 1, this go-to chapter for trials, tells us to ask God for wisdom. James invites us to ask God and encourages us that when we do ask God that He will give generously (wisdom/insight) without reproach! That's exactly what we see Jesus do, repeatedly. Can I encourage you to draw near to God amid your difficulty? Ask your honest questions and pour out your heart. Joy will follow! Psalm 30:5b says, "Weeping may tarry for the night, but joy comes with the morning."

Choose to Communicate Respectfully

Ephesians 4:29

The single biggest problem in communication is the illusion that it has taken place.

GEORGE BERNARD SHAW

As the entire family was packed into the SUV and we were driving from Chicago to Hilton Head Island for vacation, I noticed a dark, full-size car in front of me that had white spots all over it, resembling a reversed Dalmatian. I couldn't help myself, as curiosity got the best of me, and I began gaining speed to pass the car so I could get a closer look at its unique paint job. As the car was at my side it became obvious to me that it didn't have a weird paint job at all but rather was covered with gigantic bird droppings from bumper to bumper. This triggered an infantile response on my part as I reverted back to my junior high years and shouted out to everyone in our vehicle, "Look, that car is covered with crap!" followed by outbursts of uncontrollable laughter on my part, then the others'. So I kept going—even though I knew we didn't use that word in our family. "That's the crappiest car I've ever seen." I just couldn't stop myself as I was on a roll. I continued to use this unspoken word over and over again in a variety of creative ways while my three young girls perked up in the back seat. They were now laughing hysterically. I assumed they were laughing with me, but maybe they were laughing at me? They looked out the windows at this car covered with you-know-what. I started slowing down to let the you-know-what car pass me, then I would speed up and pass the you-know-what car. I did this over and over again so that everyone could get a second, third, and finally a fourth look, all the while inventing new ways to shout this apparently no-longer-forbidden word in our family to the girls as they continued to burst at the seams.

While still enjoying this moment, one opportunistic child asked the obvious question that Jody was expecting and I was oblivious to. She said, "Dad, is it all right for us to say that word too? Because Mom doesn't let us say that word." Without thinking anything of it, or consulting the well-spoken and godly copilot sitting next to me, I just blurted the word out again. Before Jody could get a word in edgewise, I had opened the door to the adjective that would become the most used word on this family vacation over the next week. It described everything from the rest stop that came next, the movie playing in the car later, the hotel accommodations that night, the not-so-great pizza place for dinner, as well as the sixteen-hour ride back home.

Maybe that story resonates with you and you have a similar one. We still laugh about that spotted-car vacation drive to this day—even if my wife was right about the fact that I shouldn't have been teaching my young children to use that word.

Most people understand (especially married people!) that the words we choose *to say* or the words we choose *not to say* have a great and lasting impact. That's the focus of this chapter, as I want to share with you what Jody and I have come to call the Ten Commandments of Healthy Communication. These will help us to understand and apply choice #6, choosing to communicate respectfully, which is obviously something I was *not* doing in the car that day.

Commandment 1: Thou Shalt Speak Truthfully

Commandment number 1 is *thou shalt speak truthfully*. As we play off the original Ten Commandments in the Bible, it seems obvious that this should be the first commandment in healthy communication. Let's discover the reason that's listed in Ephesians 4:15–16: "Rather, *speaking the truth in love*, we are to grow up in every way into him who is the head, into Christ, from whom the whole body, joined and held together by every joint with which it is equipped, when each part is working properly, makes the body grow so that it builds itself up in love" (emphasis added).

Speaking the truth in love helps us to mature and grow up properly. If we choose not to be truthful with our spouses and others, then we will never reach spiritual manhood and womanhood. Instead, we'd remain spiritual toddlers, with little aim and purpose as we foolishly deceive ourselves and those around us. That's the picture painted as we are called "to grow up in every way into him who is the head, into Christ."

Failing to accomplish this leaves us immature, underdeveloped, stagnant and stuck when it comes to our spiritual understanding and connectedness to each other. Let me share three interesting and somewhat alarming communication patterns in the typical marriage.

- On average, married couples communicate only twenty-seven minutes per week.
- The most exchanges that happen between couples are on the third date.
- The most exchanges that happen between married couples occur during the year before they get divorced.[1]

Over time, we can fall into the trap of talking less and less about the personal and intimate aspects of our lives. Speaking truthfully in love certainly means that we correct falsehoods and don't mislead our

127

spouse with lies, but it also entails that we commit to honesty and transparency. Rather, we are committed to being open and honest concerning the major and minor details of our lives, getting into the habit of intentionally carving time out each day and week in order to get caught up on the random and necessary details, like pickup and drop-off times for the kids, but also the more intimate thoughts of our hearts, minds, and souls. Jody and I touch base regularly as we do our best to meet daily before or after work and weekly on my day off to make sure we are on the same page when it comes to the necessary details and the needed and expected desires of our hearts. Sometimes it's a meeting where we need to pull the phones out to make sure our calendars are all synced up, while in other instances it's opening up our hearts with what we are thinking, learning, and experiencing.

One of the things I've made a habit of doing throughout our marriage is to make sure Jody feels like she is the first to know of the good things that are happening to me. Instead of having her be the last to know of something significant and special, I want her to be the first to know, as this communicates how much she means to me. Sometimes that means simply sending a quick text or voicemail. But it's just one simple way to confirm the priority of our relationship. Remember, it's not always the big things but more often the little things that can have the greatest impact. As we create the culture of speaking lovingly and truthfully with our spouse, let's commit to honesty in all things.

Commandment 2: Thou Shalt Choose Words Carefully

The second commandment is *thou shalt choose words carefully*. Notice what it says in Ephesians 4:29: "Let no corrupting talk come out of your mouths, but *only such as is good for building up*, as fits the occasion, that it may give grace to those who hear" (emphasis added).

We must be extremely careful when choosing our words as they can have an everlasting impact on those who hear them.

We live directly across the street from an elementary school. One day I was on the back patio studying and, although it may be hard to believe, I was working on the material for this chapter. I suddenly heard a woman screaming at the top of her lungs at her child. She and her kid were having a major meltdown during early drop-off around 8:30 in the morning and I could hear the entire exchange as it echoed from the school to my backyard. The tone and the topic was heart wrenching as the mom screamed at her daughter, "I'm so sick of this!" Then she shouted, "This happens every morning as you put up this same fight!"

I could see the mom standing in the street with her car running as she was obviously irritated and running late. The grade-school girl was upset and not wanting to go in to school. The mom put an end to it finally by yelling, "Stop crying! And get in there or else!" The girl reluctantly walked into the school as the mom got into her car and sped away.

> We must learn the importance of guarding against abusive language, especially with the most vulnerable among us.

Please hear me. I know we as parents have all been in the place were impatience, frustration, and annoyance have gotten the best of us. In the heat of the moment we may have either said some things or done some things that we would later regret. We must learn the importance of weighing our words and guarding against harsh and abusive language—especially when communicating with the most vulnerable among us. It can happen with our kids, spouses, others who are close to us, and even complete strangers.

The sad truth is that many of the grown men I have counseled are still haunted by the harsh words spoken to them by a parent. Thankfully, that was not my experience. I can remember from my earliest memories my mother telling me, "Ronnie, you're going to be a leader someday. You're going to do great things, I can see it in you, you will be a great leader."

She would say it over and over at different times and places as she

129

saw something in me that I didn't even see in myself. As I heard it, I began to believe it, as she was speaking a future reality in me. If you're reading this and some not-so-great things, to say it nicely, are still echoing in your head, disparaging, hurtful and untrue things that were said to you by someone you love, I understand that it's very difficult to erase these words from your mind. But God promises to make all things new. Just dwell on the truth that you are known and loved by God, and as the Bible declares in Romans 8:1:

> There is therefore now no condemnation for those who are in Christ Jesus.

And in 2 Corinthians 5:17:

> Therefore, if anyone is in Christ, he is a new creation. The old has passed away; behold, the new has come.

Commandment 3: Thou Shalt Follow the Spirit Wholeheartedly

Read closely Paul's exhortation in Ephesians 4:30: "Do not *grieve the Holy Spirit of God*, by whom you were sealed for the day of redemption" (emphasis added).

Not only can we grieve the Spirit with our actions and attitudes, we can also do it with our words. It's interesting that while the apostle Paul is writing this letter to encourage healthy communication within the church body, he brings up the Holy Spirit of God, the third person of the Trinity. What does it mean to "grieve" the Spirit? The Bible mentions three specific things we can do to bring grief to the Holy Spirit.

First, as mentioned here, we can "grieve the Spirit," which decreases His effectiveness in our lives. We grieve the Holy Spirit when we persist in patterns of unhealthy and unholy communication with our spouses and others in our lives. We render Him useless with our unwholesome speech and the Spirit becomes unproductive in our lives.

Secondly, 1 Thessalonians 5:19 warns us that we can "quench the Spirit." Imagine a faucet open fully with water coming out full blast. But the flow is cut off when the line is pinched or blocked completely. Similarly, this is what we do to the Spirit in our lives when we don't hear and heed what the Bible commands regarding healthy communication.

Lastly, the apostle Paul commands us in Ephesians 5:18 to "be filled with the Spirit." That means allowing the Holy Spirit full control over our thoughts, emotions, affections, and words. We're not to grieve the Spirit, nor quench the Spirit; rather, we are to be filled with the Spirit so that we can walk in the Spirit. We must speak truthfully and choose our words carefully by following the Spirit wholeheartedly.

Commandment 4: Thou Shalt Listen Intently

For the next three commandments we will look again to James 1. This time, we'll move forward to verse 19 to address the commandment *thou shalt listen intently.* James 1:19-20 reads, "Know this, my beloved brothers: let every person be *quick to hear*, slow to speak, slow to anger; for the anger of man does not produce the righteousness of God" (emphasis added). I must listen intently, or be quick to listen.

> Listen and then listen some more.

Let me share a word directly to the husbands. For you, this means eliminating ALL distractions and making eye contact with your wife when she is speaking to you. Listen and then listen some more.

Proverbs 18:13 declares: "If one gives an answer before he hears, it is his folly and shame."

Often, we speak too quickly without listening intently. This is a battle for me and for every verbal person or verbal processor. So, we need to be careful that we don't interrupt when listening. Sometimes I'll ask for Jody's opinion or perspective on a topic that I have put more time and thought into than she has. Unfortunately, she's already at an unfair disadvantage. The better approach is to give her my thoughts and then allow her time to process hers. Then later we can come back and have a meaningful conversation. I've learned the value of being a better listener. Being heard and understood is one of the most valuable gifts we can give to one another, and it costs us nothing.

Peter Drucker, the famous management guru, taught something in the business world that is extremely applicable to our marriages. He wrote, "The most important thing in communication is hearing what is *not said*." That's a mic drop moment for sure! Are you listening for what is *not being said* by your spouse? Are you taking the time to pick up on those cues? Can you read your spouse's body language and non-verbal cues? Listening intently is an art to be developed and a skill to learn as it communicates both love and respect for our spouse.

Commandment 5: Thou Shalt Respond Slowly

The fifth commandment is *thou shalt respond slowly*. This commandment ties closely to the fourth commandment, "thou shalt listen intently." It flows from the latter part of James 1:19: "Be quick to hear, *slow to speak*" (emphasis added).

Let me break that down for you in the original language. The New Testament was written in what's referred to as Koine Greek. The words translated "*slow to speak*" literally mean "*Slo-o-o-o-o-w*," "*t-o-o-o*," "*Spe-e-e-e-ak*."

Seriously now, you don't need to be in higher education or biblical scholarship to understand that. Basically, it means to resist the urge to speak. Plain and simple. Remember that cartoon "Road Runner"? When it comes to conversations in your home, stop leaving everyone in the dust like the Road Runner, with your fast talking and quick wit. Offer to the one who processes his or her thoughts some time to think the conversation through.

Let me illustrate this principle by describing two extremes. The first extreme is what I refer to as "No Filter Frieda." Or how about "Diarrhea Dan," so that we don't just single out the ladies? This is the person who says whatever he or she thinks without considering how it will affect others. From private conversations and comments to family secrets, it all comes out. You don't ever wonder what's on this person's mind because it's an open book. They reveal everything without considering the effects or audience.

The other extreme is what I call "Silent Sam." Or, so the men don't feel picked on, as they can at times be less verbal, how about "Hushed Harriet." This is the person who finds it extremely difficult to express herself. Especially when feeling attacked, Hushed Harriet is going to shut down. Sometimes it's a result of some past embarrassment or hurt as they have put themselves out on multiple occasions only to have their opinions and feelings shut down insensitively. Other times it's a result of being self-conscious, nervous, or insecure. Either way, they are hesitant to speak up and would rather let everyone else talk as they just listen in.

But it's important to understand which end of those two extremes you and your spouse gravitate to and why. Then, we each need to take a faith risk and step toward the center to communicate more effectively and respectfully.

Commandment 6: Thou Shalt Calm Down Quickly

We can't afford to minimize or gloss over what comes next in this verse, as it's part of the formula for communicating respectfully. Let's look again at James 1:19 in its entirety:

> Know this, my beloved brothers: let every person be quick to hear, slow to speak, slow to anger.

If you have a short fuse and your blood boils too quickly, then pay attention to this commandment. Your spouse and family are desperately desiring you to learn and apply this more

Losing your cool doesn't help you to advance the kingdom of God in your home.

133

consistently and regularly. The formula for removing the frustration you feel lies in commandments 4 and 5. You need to listen intently, "be quick to hear," and respond slowly, "be slow to speak," so that you can calm down quickly, "be slow to anger." James points out that our anger never brings about the righteousness God desires.

When you respond inappropriately because of being hot under the collar, it doesn't produce a good result; rather, it usually shuts down communication. Losing your cool doesn't help you to advance the kingdom of God in your home. In fact, it produces a powerfully negative impact on the kingdom. It has the same effect in your own heart as it hinders the advancement of the kingdom of God there too! It will drain and drown you and emotionally harm those you love as they cower in fear.

Jody has really helped me over the years to identify what we call the trigger points. What do I mean? These are the things that trigger that emotion of anger inside of you. I've gone so far at certain times and seasons to actually write them down so that I could identify and see the recurring patterns in order to respond appropriately. As this has been an area of growth for me, allow me to share with you what I've learned are some of the most common triggers: 1) When you feel let down or unappreciated, 2) When you feel like people are expecting too much from you, 3) When you can't accomplish a particular goal or objective, 4) When you or someone else is treated unjustly or unfairly, 5) When you feel lonely or misunderstood, 6) When things don't go smoothly and you feel pressured, annoyed, or frustrated, 7) When you feel tired and/or hungry. Hunger is sometimes referred to as "hanger" in our family, as it can be a real issue in our house at times. We all know in our own families which specific family members cannot operate on an empty stomach!

Finding a way to manage your tendency to burst out in anger is critically important for the long-term health of your marriage—and the spiritual legacy in your home. Go take a walk. Spend much time in prayer asking the Lord to guard your words. Sometimes we need to give ourselves a time-out before we speak. Some individuals may need professional counseling to weed out the deeper, more emotional issues at play. No matter the case, do whatever it takes to manage the anger.

When it controls you, it displays itself in that nasty tone, that raised voice that cuts like a knife. When you control it, you are exercising James 1:19, training yourself to listen closely, speak reservedly, and respond respectfully.

Commandment 7: Thou Shalt Humble Thyself Regularly

The seventh commandment is *thou shalt humble thyself regularly*. It's found in Matthew 7:3. Matthew records Jesus' words on this topic:

> "Why do you see the speck that is in your brother's eye, but do not notice the log that is in your own eye?"

Jesus employed an amazingly simple turn of phrase to urge His listeners off the lethal edge of relational judgment. When conflict arises in our marriage, Jesus teaches us the value of focusing on our own sinful attitude rather than what we perceive to be wrong with our spouse. That takes a great deal of humility.

Clearly, in most marital conflict both spouses share the blame. But acknowledging my own fault defuses the issue and allows for a faster resolution. Pride tempts us to refuse this Christ-honoring approach. But choosing to communicate respectfully requires making a commitment to focus on my issues, not my spouse's. It may look something like this as you and your spouse ask some important questions:

- Who will *be the first* to admit wrong?
- Who will *be the first to* apologize?
- Who will *be the first* to stand down and admit sin?
- Who will *be the first* to ask for forgiveness?
- Who will *be the first* to forgo their tendency to attack?

When it comes to your marriage: *your speck is always a log, and your spouse's log is always the speck.* That's how all of us need to see it! And if you embrace this truth, it can get you through a lot of conflict and chaos. Choosing to communicate respectfully usually requires a relational risk. The risk is humbling yourself—putting yourself out there for the good of the relationship.

Commandment 8: Thou Shalt Withhold Words Appropriately

The eighth commandment is that *thou shalt withhold words appropriately.* We've touched on this a bit already in the third commandment as we talked about choosing your words carefully. However, as we continue to read from Matthew 7 we see this truth from a slightly different angle.

Jesus gave a compelling warning about the negative use of words in Matthew 7:6:

> "Do not give dogs what is holy, and do not throw your pearls before pigs, lest they trample them underfoot and turn to attack you."

Jesus makes plain the importance of investing your most valuable communication in someone who will appreciate it and embrace it in a worthy manner. The opposite of that is investing such intimacy in someone who carelessly disregards such virtuous expression and tosses it aside like pig slop. That's the idea. This is a helpful principle that applies to all types of conversations and relationships, even between husband and wife, as there are times when it's more powerful to just say nothing at all.

A good example is when we have opportunity to share our faith with an unbeliever. When I responded the first time to hearing the gospel, my heart was extremely open and receptive because of what was happening in my life. I had to fall to look up. Others would say they had to come to the end of themselves, which many in our marriage conferences have experienced. Adverse circumstances of life ripen people to the gospel message. Hearts can be made much more open to your words of help and hope during times of heartache and failure. Such divine interruptions can get people thinking introspectively and eternally about the real meaning and purpose of life.

Please hear my heart in this section as all of us rub shoulders with people who are enduring the weight this life brings whether it's family, friends, coworkers, neighbors, or even brief acquaintances. Take advantage of these opportunities, as people need your guidance and prayers as you point them to the One who can lift them from despair. Even if you can't identify with their specific struggle, you can always identify with how it feels to be hopeless.

Say something like, "Thanks for sharing your situation with me, and although I can't identify with your specific struggle, God has met me during my most difficult times and He wants to do the same for you."

Now, back to Matthew 7:6 and how it applies to marriage. Remember Jesus warns, "Do not give dogs what is holy, and do not throw your pearls before pigs, lest they trample them underfoot and turn to attack you." It's important to realize as a spouse that you don't have to win every argument and you don't always have to have the last word. To communicate respectfully there are times when you need to hold your tongue and not say a word. Often, that's the most powerful thing you could possibly do. I've heard it said, "Be careful with your words; once they are said they can only be forgiven, not forgotten."

> **It's important to realize as a spouse that you don't have to win every argument.**

I could not agree more with that statement!

Commandment 9: Thou Shalt Seek Help When Necessary

The ninth commandment is *thou shalt seek help when necessary*. I want to look to a passage of Scripture that is most often turned to when the subject of church discipline arises in churches. Unfortunately, it often goes overlooked and underutilized when it comes to showing people the biblical support of seeking the counsel of others through relational breakdown and strife. It teaches us the important biblical principles as we confront each other over potential sin issues or general misunderstandings. Jesus shows us the path to follow so that it gets handled in the best way and is blessed by God. The passage is found in Matthew 18:15–20:

> "If your brother sins against you, go and tell him his fault, between you and him alone. If he listens to you, you have gained your brother. But if he does not listen, take one or two others along with you, that every charge may be established by the evidence of two or three witnesses. If he refuses to listen to them, tell it to the church. And if he refuses to listen even to the church, let him be to you as a Gentile and a tax collector. Truly, I say to you, whatever you bind on earth shall be bound in heaven, and whatever you loose on earth shall be loosed in heaven. Again I say to you, if two of you agree on earth about anything they ask, it will be done for them by my Father in heaven. For where two or three are gathered in my name, there am I among them."

In this great passage, I see three stages to help us in most types of relational reconciliation. I personally like to think of them as stages rather than steps because each stage could possibly have more than one meeting to come together to a mutual understanding. Sometimes each stage will require more time and attention than planned, as you don't want to rush the process to jump to the next stage. I've learned that it's better to be careful and cautious in situations like this rather than to rush quickly to judgment.

STAGE ONE: Meet individually. This meeting happens when a person has a direct issue with another person whether that turns out to be a sin issue, some unfortunate misunderstanding, or a blind spot in their life. That's why it's best if you can meet face-to-face to try and resolve the conflict. Trust me, it's always the best step to talk "to" the person directly rather than talk "about" the person indirectly to others. If the person who is confronted with the problem listens, then you're on your way to reconciliation. But if the person refuses to listen, then the next stage is necessary.

STAGE TWO: Bring along a mature and trusted friend. Having a third individual adds force but also brings another layer of accountability and perhaps a fresh perspective. If the person still isn't listening and continues to refuse any input or counsel, then the next stage is essential.

STAGE THREE: Bring the individual to the wider community of faith—the church. The third stage involves the church as you invite a pastor or ministry leader into the process to help identify a plan to move forward that serves not only the individuals but the church family as well.

The key to benefiting from the principles in this passage, as we focus in on marriage relationships, lies in the phrase that's used two times in the positive—"if he [she] listens"—and two times in the negative—"if he [she] does not listen." If the person listens, then you're on your way to working things out and you don't need to move on to the next stage. If the person does not listen, then you need to move on to the next stage.

Listening reveals an open and repentant heart that is humbly willing to learn and grow. Not listening reveals a potentially hardened and unrepentant heart that is unwilling to learn and grow. As Jody and I have been involved in helping and counseling couples over the years, we've seen great maturity and growth in those who are willing to listen and learn from each other. Sometimes it's not easy to get to this place as others are brought in to give advice and counsel. But either way it is necessary to involve others when you need help or when you are stuck in a stalemate. Be careful not to exile yourselves as individuals or as a couple. Instead, surround yourselves with godly, loving people who can safely and compassionately speak into your life. From trusted and mature friends to pastors and counselors, make sure you don't walk alone. Don't be embarrassed to seek the help of others, especially during marital breakdown. God's people are uniquely (divinely!) equipped to help you experience the breakthrough your relationship deserves and desires. Make sure to do your part in keeping your heart open and pliable before the Lord. Then He can use the wisdom of others to bring the health, healing, and hope you and your marriage need.

Commandment 10: Thou Shalt Purify Thyself Continually

The tenth commandment is *thou shalt purify thyself continually*. Keeping pure needs to happen inside all of us regularly. This principle again comes directly from Jesus' lips as He declares it in Matthew 15:17-20:

> "Do you not see that whatever goes into the mouth passes into the stomach and is expelled? But what comes out of the mouth proceeds from the heart, and this defiles a person. For out of the heart come evil thoughts, murder, adultery, sexual immorality, theft, false witness, slander. These are what defile a person. But to eat with unwashed hands does not defile anyone."

You may be wondering what Jesus means in these words. He's obviously not talking about what you ate for breakfast or lunch yesterday. Jesus is referring to the condition of your heart. The heart must be pure always. That's such an important principle in strengthening the marriage knot. The impure heart expresses things that aren't nice and does things that are wrong. It's not about the external but the internal, from bad thoughts to murder and everything in between. The blame shifting, swearing, lying, cheating, and self-righteous attitudes—all flow from an unclean heart.

Any parent who's gotten through the teenage years learns that it's not the behavior that's the real issue, but rather what lies deep inside.

That's always where it all starts and that's always what needs to be addressed. The behavior is only the symptom while the unclean heart or deceived heart is the real problem. The question to figure out is what's driving the behavior or motivating them to act out in this way.

The prophet Jeremiah reminds us in Jeremiah 17:9:

> The heart is deceitful above all things,
>> and desperately sick;
>> who can understand it?

That means our hearts can't be trusted because they can become so deceitful, defiled, and dirty. When someone gives you the wisdom of the world by saying, "just follow your heart," they are counseling you contrary to God's Word. Jesus appeals to the inward desires and motivations of the heart. Every heart needs to be power-washed by the grace and mercy of God. That's the only solution. And I wish it was a onetime deal, but just as you need to brush your teeth each day to keep them clean and sparkly white, you also need to purify your heart each day.

But long before you can maintain a pure heart, you must be given a new heart—a spiritual heart—by God. That's what happens when you surrender your life by faith to Jesus Christ. He creates in you a clean and pure heart (2 Cor. 5:17). It starts with open heart surgery as you get a brand-new heart, spiritually speaking, when you embrace Jesus Christ as Savior and Lord.

Ezekiel 36:26 tells us that God wants to replace that "heart of stone" with a "heart of flesh" that beats for Him. So that's the first thing. Secondly, it begins to be purified as you grow in your relationship with God as you read the Word, pray, fast, go to church, serve, and daily confess your sin and walk by faith. These are the ancient paths we must follow. The Bible is the fuel for the other disciplines, so make sure you get yourself into the regular habit of reading and meditating on God's Word. Remember that following God isn't about pursuing the latest fad or newest trend but rather walking with God down ancient, well-worn paths. Jeremiah 6:16 declares,

> Thus says the LORD:
> "Stand by the roads, and look,
>   and ask for the ancient paths,
>   where the good way is; and walk in it,
>   and find rest for your souls."

Husbands and wives, that's the benefit of purifying ourselves continually as we walk these ancient paths together and exercise the spiritual disciplines. There is healing on that path and rest for your weary and struggling marriage.

Proverbs 4:23 says:

> Keep your heart with all vigilance,
>   for from it flow the springs of life.

We need to guard our hearts when it comes to healthy communication. Let's make sure we follow the 10 commandments to healthy communication as we speak truthfully, choose our words carefully, follow the spirit wholeheartedly, listen intently, respond slowly, calm down quickly, humble ourselves regularly, withhold words appropriately, seek help when necessary, and purify ourselves continually.

A helpful exercise to end this chapter is to take a few moments to read James 3:1–12 below, perhaps with your spouse. After you do, ask God to help you use your words in ways that build up your spouse and others around you as you choose to communicate respectfully.

James 3:1–12

> Not many of you should become teachers, my brothers, for you know that we who teach will be judged with greater strictness. For we all stumble in many ways. And if anyone does not stumble in what he says, he is a perfect man, able also to bridle

his whole body. If we put bits into the mouths of horses so that they obey us, we guide their whole bodies as well. Look at the ships also: though they are so large and are driven by strong winds, they are guided by a very small rudder wherever the will of the pilot directs. So also the tongue is a small member, yet it boasts of great things.

How great a forest is set ablaze by such a small fire! And the tongue is a fire, a world of unrighteousness. The tongue is set among our members, staining the whole body, setting on fire the entire course of life, and set on fire by hell. For every kind of beast and bird, of reptile and sea creature, can be tamed and has been tamed by mankind, but no human being can tame the tongue. It is a restless evil, full of deadly poison. With it we bless our Lord and Father, and with it we curse people who are made in the likeness of God. From the same mouth come blessing and cursing. My brothers, these things ought not to be so. Does a spring pour forth from the same opening both fresh and salt water? Can a fig tree, my brothers, bear olives, or a grapevine produce figs? Neither can a salt pond yield fresh water.

From Jody's Heart . . .

What a great challenge from James that we need to make "how" and "what" we communicate a priority. The consequences of not doing so are devastating! How clear that we need God's help in attempting to tame the tongue as it states that "no human being can tame the tongue." Recognizing that our communication flows from our heart is key. If we want only words that are "good for building up . . . that . . . give grace to those who hear" (Eph. 4:29), it seems to me that our hearts need to be filled with God's love, His truth, and encouraging words. This is a challenge because we also learn that by nature our hearts are deceitful. How do we ensure that what is flowing from poor hearts are the real life-giving building-up words versus the ones that are "setting on fire the entire course of life, and [are] set on fire by hell"?

What a contrast! The best way I know how to put out a fire is to either drench it with water or snuff it out by smothering the flame. This makes me think about how we were challenged in this chapter to be "filled with the Holy Spirit" instead of quenching the Spirit with bad stuff that comes out of our hearts and mouths. So, what if we focus on asking and inviting the Holy Spirit to "fill" our hearts which is like drenching with pure water the words and thoughts that set forests ablaze? In turn, instead of quenching the Holy Spirit, focus on quenching the pride, deceit, and bitterness in our hearts. We need God's help to do these things, which is okay because He wants to do these things in us. He loves when we invite Him into our marriage and rely on Him to do the things that only He can do for us.

How does this play out in our marriage? Maybe we make a practice of asking God to be filled with His Spirit before we sit down to discuss a hot topic like finances or a problem with a mother-in-law? We also ask for forgiveness for the bitterness or pride in our hearts that is making this such a difficult thing to talk about. We pray these things together and invite God to give us the words to communicate the truth in love. We pray that our words would be seasoned with grace. That we would have ears to hear and listen to understand. Inviting God to be in the center of our conversations should help us to ward off saying things that we will regret.

I can tell you this: We are always going to be learning to communicate respectfully. It's an ongoing daily practice. We will screw up when we are practicing and learning something hard or new. That's allowed! Own it, admit when you know you're wrong, ask for forgiveness, and get back at it! Give grace to each other. Be quick to forgive and even quicker to admit when you're wrong. And most importantly, invite God, His Holy Spirit, into your heart and mind to help you communicate respectfully. Let Him do this in you!

Time out! Are you communicating in a respectful way with your spouse? Could your communication patterns use an upgrade? Rate your communication online at **Ronzappia.com/communicationassessment**

Choose to Bless Abundantly
Proverbs 3:27

Those who are happiest are those who do the most for others.

BOOKER T. WASHINGTON

While my mom was struggling with cancer I wrote a tribute that summarized my thoughts and feelings about her, and what she meant to me growing up. I read it to her at a family gathering while she was going through the most difficult trial of her life. It is entitled "A Tribute to an Awesome Mom." I've included it here to share some of the most valuable lessons that I learned from my mom, a woman who chose to bless abundantly.

> *Dear Mom,*
>
> I am writing to pay tribute to you. It is long overdue and I want to share with you how much your love for me has impacted my life. I'm thankful to God for your response to the phone call over thirty-five years ago informing you and dad that Catholic Charities was having a hard time placing an Italian baby, now a few months old, who needed a home. The love and respect you have shown to me has influenced me to this day. I'm grateful for a mom who always loved me and made

sacrifices for me. You laid down your own life to serve me and our family. I didn't thank you enough for all you did for us.

My childhood is filled with happy memories of a caring mother. I didn't realize how good I had it as you cooked steaks, ribs, and pizza for me whenever I wanted, no matter what you were doing. You took care of me so well, always asking what I desired and buying me whatever I needed, even the nicest clothes. So much so, that it won me "best dressed" in high school my senior year! I could always count on you to slip me some extra cash on my way back to college too. Mom, you did the little things to make me feel special, to let me know I was loved. You taught me that love is not a passing emotion or some distant feeling but a willingness to do for another. Your marriage to dad is a picture to me of faithfulness, devotion, and kindness. You had respect for dad and showed it in so many ways, always complimenting him and speaking so highly of him.

Your friendship with dad and love for him has been a model for our marriage today. I always remember the two of you joining hands at any age and always enjoying being together. You just don't see two people persevere through trials and adversity of life these days. You honored each other, laughed together, and served each other so faithfully for forty-nine years. Your commitment to marriage honored God and taught me more than you'll ever know.

As I remember you I think of six simple words:

Hilarious

You always have had such a great sense of humor. Whether it was sticking your tongue out at some jerk on the highway, which I do remember, or throwing a dinner roll at me when I simply asked to pass the bread at the supper table. You always made me laugh. Jody says I get my sense of humor and hilarious side from you.

Compassionate

You have a huge heart for family. You put the family first above all else. You always worked to get our family and extended family together. Always looking to give of yourself to relatives and friends. You took care of grandma and pretty much every other elderly person on her street. You couldn't walk by someone who had a need without trying to meet it. People of this world may say you were gullible, but Jesus called it compassion. And then there's my family. Jody and I didn't buy our girls any clothes when they were young because you bought them everything. Your generosity and heart for others will never be forgotten by me. I pray that I will care for those around me as much as you cared for strangers.

Valuable

You saw the value in everything. What others could not see you would see. Whether it was an antique or an unbelievable piece of memorabilia, you bought it or saved it, refinished it or restored it, and had a place for it. You loved to collect antiques and tell the stories about each piece. I'm grateful for all those you gave us as they remind me of you and I love them too.

Adventurous

In the kitchen you could cook up anything. You searched everywhere and found our house in Kirtland and made it a home. You mixed cement with the construction workers when we did the addition for our home in Euclid. You were always willing to do whatever was needed and go anywhere in a moment's notice. You were not too tired to play baseball in the driveway with your grandson, Allen. . . . You always got the best deal at TJ Maxx. You could shop longer than any other human being at Gurnee Mills Mall. You never passed a pawnshop you didn't visit. . . . Memories I will never forget!

Security

You were always there for me. No matter what happened or what trouble would come, I could always count on your presence and smile. You always made yourself available to me and were faithful to look after me. You never asked for anything, but instead always asked what I wanted. I could always count on your love and could always feel secure in your arms. I hope that I can model this to my children.

Smart

Smart enough to know that there is more than this life. The Bible teaches that this life is like a vapor when compared to eternity. Smart enough to know that there is nothing you can do to earn your way to heaven. Smart enough to understand that just as a child trusts in their earthly father to protect them, you must trust in your heavenly Father to protect you. Smart enough to believe that Jesus Christ died on the cross to pay for your sins, and rose again to give new life. Smart enough to place your faith and trust in Him. Smart enough to embrace Him as your personal Savior and Lord a year and a half ago. Mom, you have a teachable spirit. Jesus said in John 10:27-28, "My sheep hear my voice, and I know them, and they follow me. I give them eternal life, and they will never perish, and no one will snatch them out of my hand."

I love you, Mom, and Jesus loves you much more.

Your son,

Ron

I'll never forget how meaningful this tribute was to my mom when I read it to her, as well as the reaction that it brought when I shared it at her funeral. Many came to believe in Jesus that day. As we continue to talk about strengthening the marriage knot, I want us to remember that waiting to bless would be a deadly mistake. The example I want others to follow is not of me but of my mom who chose to bless so naturally, moment to moment, day after day, year after year! That's the target we are aiming for in this last of seven choices to strengthen your marriage: *Choose to bless abundantly*. Once again, the Old Testament wisdom of Proverbs will be our guide.

The First Way: Bless Your Spouse Practically

Proverbs 11:25 says,

> Whoever brings blessing will be enriched.

Then look at what it says next.

> [The] one who waters [that's the one who is doing the blessing] will himself be watered.

Why should we choose to bless other people? There are benefits not only to the other person, but also to you. It not only helps them practically, but it also blesses us immensely.

So what does it look like "to bless" your spouse practically? The Hebrew word for blessing literally has the idea of "kneeling down" for the other person. In his bestselling book *The 5 Love Languages®*, Gary Chapman outlines the five ways we can express and prefer to receive love from our mates. Here they are for you to consider:

- Words of affirmation
- Acts of service
- Physical touch
- Quality time
- Gifts

These languages are outlined in this go-to book, and have become a guide to understanding the primary way that each of us desire to be loved. (Go to www.5lovelanguages.com to take the assessment online.)

Do you know what your spouse's love language is? Are you consistently loving him or her in this way? If not, there is an unnecessary disconnect as you may be doing a good thing, but not the best thing.

During the early years, which spanned a good five-year period for us, it was all about quality time for Jody. Then, we had children and everything changed! You might not be surprised, like I was, that her love language changed to "acts of service." She felt most loved by me when I picked up some of the required tasks of raising kids and maintaining a busy home. Then, during our kids' teen years, it changed back to her go-to language "quality time," sprinkled with some "words of affirmation," I think, to just keep me on my toes!

Learn from my experience, husbands, because our experience is not unique. Your wife's love language can change during the different seasons of life. In case you're wondering, I'm still always digging on gifts though! Learn the best ways to practically bless your spouse in each season of life. That's the principle in view.

The Second Way: Bless Your Spouse Prayerfully

The second way is to *bless your spouse prayerfully*. Look at Proverbs 15:29:

> The LORD is far from the wicked,
>> but he hears the prayer of the righteous.

I love this principle. Pray for your spouse—regularly and passionately. God's waiting. God's listening, God wants to hear from you. God wants you to call out to Him. And He will unleash His power, protection, and provision in the life of your mate as He responds to your prayer.

Let me ask you a couple of quick questions. How often do you pray *for* your spouse? How often do you pray *with* your spouse? Studies show that if you do choose to pray together at least once a day, your divorce rate goes down to less than one percent![1] Prayer is not optional; prayer is essential.

Why should we pray? Good question. I offer five helpful reasons:

- **Prayer Helps**: Prayer helps you, your marriage, and your family as you invite the power of God to bear weight on every situation.

- **Prayer Humbles**: There's something about praying with your spouse or with your kids that puts you in a place of humility as you sincerely express your dependence and need for God.

- **Prayer Heals**: Prayer can heal us and those around us physically, spiritually, and emotionally. It may not take away all the pain instantly or forever, but it will get you *through* the pain for now as you invite the Healer and Comforter into your situation.

- **Prayer Hopes**: Through prayer, we find encouragement when we are discouraged, contentment when we are anxious, and hope when we are despairing. Prayer is the greenhouse of hope!

- **Prayer Honors**: Praying for and with your spouse will honor God as you acknowledge His sovereignty, recognize His attributes, and depend on His strength and power. It will honor your spouse as you go before God together, praising Him and calling on Him for your deepest needs, and thanking Him. It creates an intimacy that precious few will ever experience.

As you pray together as a couple, you're putting yourself in a good place and you're putting God in His place of authority as you submit your marriage and family to Him. Ask your spouse how you can be praying for him or her regularly. Bless your spouse prayerfully.

The Third Way: Bless Your Spouse Verbally

The third way is to bless your spouse verbally. We've touched on this extensively in choice number 6, *choose to communicate respectfully.* However, Proverbs 18:21 doubles down on what we've already learned:

> Death and life are in the power of the tongue,
> and those who love it will eat its fruits.

What does this mean? It means our words have extreme power. Our words can lift, encourage, strengthen, and give life to the most brokenhearted among us; our words can also tear down, damage, and even destroy a life. The tongue is a very small but potent thing, as we have learned already, like the bit in a horse's mouth or the rudder of a ship (James 3:3-4). Whether it's leaving a necessary note of instruction on the counter with a big heart drawn on it, a card on the dresser for no reason other than to say, "I love you," or playing a familiar love song that you start singing in the car as it plays off your playlist. Choose to bless your spouse verbally every day.

The Fourth Way: Bless Your Spouse Romantically

The fourth way is to bless your spouse romantically. Look closely at Proverbs 21:16:

> One who wanders from the way of good sense
> will rest in the assembly of the dead.

Husbands, some of you have a relationship that is on life support because you're not romancing your wife. Your marriage needs some resuscitation. When you bless your spouse romantically, it provides the boost needed to roll back the calendar and get back to the good old days.

I remember our wedding night. Jody and I were married on the east side of Cleveland. I surprised her by renting a stretch limo that drove us into the city as a nightcap. I'll never forget that thirty-minute drive as we drove downtown, and then the detour through "The Flats" as we were standing up in the car through the sunroof. We had a reservation at the nicest hotel in town (which just so happened to be the only nice hotel in town, at that time), near Terminal Tower. I was able to get the nicest room because a friend of a friend was the manager, and he just happened to be working the front desk when we arrived. To our great surprise he gave us an "upgrade" that we will never forget. He handed us the keys to the Presidential Suite on the top floor. The place was bigger than our first home!

Before we checked out, I looked at Jody who was so cheerful and happy, but she could see the disappointment in my face. She innocently asked what was wrong as we just had the time of our lives staying in the penthouse of this posh hotel. I replied hesitantly, "Honey, I'm sorry." She said, "Why, what could you be sorry about after all this?" And I replied, "Because that's the nicest place we will *ever* stay in our lives and it's probably going to be all downhill from here!"

Blessing your spouse romantically doesn't always have to cost a lot of money. You can keep it simple and inexpensive. Most wives don't need much but are moved by their husband's genuine and loving gestures at romance. Don't take long sabbaticals away from romancing your spouse as it fans the flame and breathes life into your marriage. Bless your spouse romantically!

The Fifth Way: Bless Your Spouse Financially

The fifth way to bless your spouse is financially. Proverbs 21:20 reveals that,

> Precious treasure and oil are in a wise man's dwelling,
>   but a foolish man devours it.

Now, take a moment to consider these words. They are making a comparison between the wise person who is responsibly saving for the future and the foolish person who irresponsibly spends everything without concern for tomorrow. The underlying theme is that of provision. It's about providing for the needs of each other in the future by taking responsibility in the present day. Many marriages are strained because of a failure to manage money properly, whether it's the lack of money as couples are trying to make ends meet, or the pursuit of money as it can seem like enough is never enough. I have seen the negative effects of both as the abundance or the scarcity of money provides the fuel for continual fighting and frustration.

A recent *New York Times* poll said that if you disagree with your spouse on a regular basis and you're fighting about money, you have a 30 percent higher chance of getting divorced.[2] It's important to deal with this issue of money as couples need to be united and on the same team when it comes to finances. Let me share five rules we have followed that have helped us experience financial freedom. It's not an exhaustive list, but it will get you off to a pretty good start.

The first rule is to set a budget and stick to it. It's so important. I can't tell you how many couples we counsel that don't have a budget. If you don't have a budget, you must discipline yourself to set one. Sit down with somebody who can teach you how to do it if necessary. Communication is key, and remember, this is a team effort in marriage, to build a budget that you can both maintain and achieve.

Pay off your credit cards each month. For those who are having trouble, it's time to get serious. That new couch you're sitting on or that snazzy coat you're wearing is not worth the 18-20 percent interest payment you're saddled with. Meet with a financial planner if necessary or a seasoned couple in your church and come up with a plan to rid yourselves of credit card debt.

Live within your means. We're in a day and age of consumerism, where people get caught up feeling as if they need more and more, the best of the best, and everything right now. Resist that urge. Downsize if you must. Do things that are radical to put your marriage and your family in a solid financial place. Jody and I made a tough choice early in our marriage. Even though we both had lucrative professional jobs, we had agreed that we would live and purchase our first home based on just my income! We did this because it was our desire to have Jody stay at home someday when God blessed us with kids. She was committed to working as hard as she could and earning and saving as much money as possible so that we could do this. And that is what we did.

God has richly blessed that decision in ways we cannot even begin to describe.

Give back to God. Scripture teaches that we are to be generous givers and give a biblical portion back to God. Why? Because the truth is He owns everything! The psalmist reminds us that, "The earth is the LORD's, and everything in it" (Ps. 24:1 NIV). That means that everything you have isn't really your own as it has been given to you on consignment. From that house that you live in, to the shirt on your back, to that car that won't start, you say, "God, it's Yours. Please take it!" Even our very own kids; everything belongs to God. That helps lay the groundwork for a proper biblical understanding of stewardship so that we will be generous people and give back. I've heard it said this way: "You can't outgive God." He has blessed us in so many ways so that we can and should be a blessing.

Let me shoot straight: too many people are stingy when it comes to giving back to God and the local church. If that's you, take a step of faith and see what God does as the Scriptures tell us to test Him in this (Mal. 3:10-12). Trust me, over the years Jody and I have stretched ourselves to give more and more back to God, and we have seen and experienced the blessing in a variety of ways. Test Him. Try Him. He will be faithful.

Save a percentage of income. Too many young people I talk to are not saving enough or not saving anything at all. Their income is like a revolving door. In and out, repeatedly. You may not think that saving a small percentage of your paycheck is worth it right now, but it all adds up over time. There is power in multiplication over the years as that little bit adds up and multiplies. Do you have a matching program at your work? Are you taking advantage of it? Do everything you can to participate, as it's free money you don't want to leave on the table. We've always done this when we were in the corporate world with stock purchasing plans, and now in ministry with our 401(k) and 403(b). When Jody and I first married, the first thing I did for her was to open an IRA so we could get started saving for the future right away.

Again, this is not an exhaustive list of rules at all, but it certainly will point you in the right direction as the Bible makes it clear that money isn't bad in and of itself; it's only "the love of money" that is bad. Bless your spouse financially by being a good steward of what God has entrusted to you.

The Sixth Way: Bless Your Spouse Spiritually

The sixth way to *bless your spouse is spiritually*. Look closely at Proverbs 21:21:

> Whoever pursues righteousness and kindness
>   will find life, righteousness, and honor.

If you've been following God for some time, you know what pursuing righteousness means. It's not about your goodness or greatness as you're trying to impress or earn favor with God. No, it's about *God's* righteousness that's found in Christ. God's imputed righteousness has been made available to us through Jesus' death. Pursuing righteousness is about pursuing a dependent relationship with Christ, the source of our righteousness. There is nothing we can do to earn salvation. It's a gift that grants us the imputed righteousness of Christ. You can't get to heaven because of your own good works or good deeds. God declares in Isaiah 64:6 that "all our righteous acts are like filthy rags" (NIV). That's clear, isn't it?

We can't restore our relationship with God on our own terms. It's only through Christ's redemptive work.

Yet God does call us as Christians to pursue righteousness by pursuing a relationship with Jesus. We're called to a Christlike lifestyle and challenged in the Scriptures to follow Him with everything we have. We need to bless our spouse spiritually by taking responsibility for our own spiritual growth in Christ. God doesn't want you to be stagnant and stuck spiritually. He desires that you climb to get to new heights of spiritual maturity.

The Bible teaches us to "strive for . . . holiness without which no one will see the Lord" (Heb. 12:14). That's a strong statement for each of us to reflect on individually, as God desires us to become more and more like His Son by spending time with His Son and thereby reflecting His attitudes and actions. Your continued growth proves who you really are spiritually. So, let's go for it. Stop with the excuses. Jesus gave it all for you; how can you settle for giving Him anything less? He's available and accessible and wants to lead and guide you through His Word, His ways, and His Holy Spirit.

Husbands, I want to challenge you. Why? Because the statistics are downright nasty. On any given Sunday, there are 13 million more women than men in church. Statistics tell us the typical church is 61 percent female and 39 percent male on a given weekend. It's like 25 percent of married women are there without their husbands. It's the wife who is there by herself. It's worse for midweek activities in the church, whether that's coming to the church or a small group or other activity, where the percentage is 70 to 80 percent women.[3] Men, where are you?

Husbands, let me give some growth rules for getting started.

Read the Bible regularly. Joshua 1:8 is clear: "This Book of the Law shall not depart from your mouth, but you shall meditate on it day and night, so that you may be careful to do according to all that is written in it. For then you will make your way prosperous, and then you will have good success." I ran across a certain Gallup Poll that has been asking the same question for years. The question is simply, what do Americans believe about the Bible? From the mid-1970s to 1984, close to 40 percent considered the Bible to be the literal word of God, but that has been declining ever since. Now, only 24 percent, or roughly one in four Americans, believe that the Bible is "the actual word of God, and to be taken literally, word for word."[4] What do you believe about the Bible? How you answer this question will stall or jumpstart your faith.

Pray with your wife frequently. James 5:16 talks about prayer and the necessity of confessing to one another. Maybe you're wondering, "Well, how often is 'regularly' and how often is 'frequently'?" Okay, how about this? Regularly and frequently means two to three times more than you're doing right now. I'm sort of joking, but not really. I think you get what I'm saying. Simply step up in your commitment to pray with her.

Attend church weekly with your family. Hebrews 10:24-25 says, "And let us consider how to stir up one another to love and good works, not neglecting to meet together, as is the habit of some." Too many people are on the monthly plan or the bimonthly plan or the no plan when it comes to church attendance, according to those previous statistics (trust me, I've been a senior pastor for almost twenty years now). And don't settle for online services all the time either! I understand that there are times when you don't have a choice, like when you're traveling or when the kids are sick. But remember what's really going on long-term is you're curating the culture your family will most likely continue. This is about establishing a spiritual legacy. That responsibility primarily falls to the man of the house.

The Seventh Way: Bless Your Spouse Faithfully

This principle flows from Proverbs 3:27:

> Do not withhold good from those to whom it is due.

Remember the old Peanuts cartoon when Charlie Brown would get ready to kick the football and Lucy would volunteer to hold it? Every time she would hold the ball and he would start running to kick it, Lucy would pull the ball away so he fell flat on his back. Charlie Brown was so trusting and Lucy was so predictable. As a kid watching this routine, I would be thinking to myself, "How can he let her do that to him again?"

Let's not treat each other in this fashion—playing games, continuing the same old routine of not working together but against each other. That's a picture of withholding good for selfish reasons. Let's stop pulling the ball away so that someone falls on their back in the marriage and you can't rally up the points for God. Whether it's a field goal or an extra point, let's run up the score by working together as husband and wife for the glory of God in our marriage and family. Let's do our part to help each other to be successful, individually and as a team. You can identify the areas in your marriage where you need to be working better together. That just takes a bit of focused time and honest communication. Once you have your list, prayerfully commit to following through for each other. Remember that God wants to strengthen your marriage as that third cord binding the two together.

Usually at our Marriage Knot Conferences, we end our time in the last session by asking married couples to bless their spouse faithfully through the renewing of their vows. We'll usually have several pastors up front as they help facilitate the process by leading them and praying for them as the couples come forward to bless each other in this way. It's always a memorable time for Jody and me as we experience the joy of watching so many couples recommit themselves to each other and the Lord. Whether it's the couple who walked in needing a minor tune-up, or the couple in need of a major overhaul, there is power in the mutual commitment they display as they reaffirm their love for God and each other.

One author reminds us, "Wedding vows are not a declaration of present love but a mutually binding promise of future love."[5]

Here are the vows that we provide the couples with as they take turns reading them to each other and then saying, "I will" as they did that very first time. I hope now that we have come to the end of these seven choices that you'll consider sharing these vows with your spouse as you continue to tighten the marriage knot. I simply ask you to read these words to your spouse after you read them over for yourself. Husbands, take the lead and initiate the process. The vows I've prepared are patterned after what we've been learning together in this book. You and your spouse will be blessed:

I know who you are and I believe in who God is making you to be. I accept you as you are and thank God for the gift you are to me. I will never knowingly neglect or forsake our marriage. Forgive me for when I have made our marriage about me or specifically my needs. God deserves the best of who we are and who we will become. I want to be your biggest encourager and your best friend born for adversity. I will make the choices necessary to tighten the marriage knot regularly and strengthen our relationship continually. I know I have failed you at times. Please be patient with me as I am a work in progress and committed to spiritual maturity and growth. I promise to be open, honest, and real with you. I will close the gap of integrity God has shown me with your help. I love you and believe in you and want to grow together in Christ with you. I want us to believe in Jesus, belong to Jesus and become like Jesus together. Will you be my partner in life as we pursue the things of God? Will you be my partner in marriage as we die to self and live for Christ? Will you be my partner in the gospel as we grow and share our faith? Will you be my partner in Christ as we do what we need to do to tighten the marriage knot?

(Together say, "I will.")

Perhaps it's time for you to take up the challenge of renewing your vows with your spouse. I would highly recommend it. And again, husbands, go ahead and take the lead for your wife. Whether you use the above words I've provided and do it informally as you grab your spouse's hand in this moment, or you stand before friends and family in a public setting, the goal is to stand firm and renew your commitment to bless one another faithfully as you do your part to tighten your marriage knot.

From Jody's Heart . . .

I truly hope at this point, you, like Ron and me, have become acutely aware that marriage was clearly designed by God, for God, and meant to be enjoyed with God. The challenges and choices we have been presenting, and hopefully you have been discussing with each other, did not come from man. These choices are how we have learned, often the hard way, to put God's plan for marriage into practice. Attempting to put something He designed into practice apart from Him will be futile. The more we invite God into our discussions about these choices (and maybe some changes we feel or know that God wants us to make), the better chance we have of implementing them and experiencing the tightening of this marriage knot and furthering our commitment to help couples stay together!

If you are like Ron and me and realize that you have been unfaithful to the commitment you made before God on your wedding day, then the choice to redo your marriage vows isn't just a suggestion, it's a necessity. I'll never forget the early spring day in the backyard of our first house when we had our marriage ministry pastor lead us in re-committing ourselves to each other. We didn't realize that it would have been a good idea to have a witness or two—we almost asked our neighbor who was taking out her garbage. Tom, our marriage ministry pastor, assured us that he and God and each other would suffice. The passage he chose was 2 Corinthians 5:17–20 which says, "Therefore, if anyone is in Christ, he is a new creation. The old has passed away; behold, the new has come. All this is from God, who through Christ reconciled us to himself and gave us the ministry of reconciliation; that is, in Christ God was reconciling the world to himself, not counting their trespasses against them, and entrusting to us the message of reconciliation. Therefore, we are ambassadors for Christ, God making his appeal through us. We implore you on behalf of Christ, be reconciled to God."

Little did we know that God was literally speaking over us the ministry of reconciliation for our lives. First, Ron has the privilege of joining God in reconciling individuals to God through the clear, concise, and effective proclamation of the way to God through faith in Jesus—the gospel. Ron gets to share this life-transforming message on a weekly basis to thousands of people as the Senior Pastor of Highpoint Church in Chicagoland, as well as through the airwaves of radio broadcasts through Highpoint Ministries. Not to mention the many people from all over who livestream or listen to podcasts nationwide. Trust me, we had no plan for any of those things that spring day in our backyard. We would have said you were insane to think that Ron would later become a pastor, never mind those other things. The only plan was that we were re-committing our lives to each other and to building our lives, our marriage, and our family on the solid Rock of Jesus and His Word.

Secondly, unbeknownst to us that day, God was giving us the ministry of reconciling husbands and wives that would years later become the foundation for the Marriage Knot conference ministry and seedbed for this book! Our hope is that the same healing and hope that we experienced when God reconciled our broken marriage knot would be known by countless other couples. Only God knew that day when we renewed our vows that He was preparing us to become "ambassadors for Christ, God making his appeal through us." Our prayer is that you and your marriage knot will be strengthened in Christ because of our time together!

Thank you for reading this book, and thank you for the privilege of allowing us to speak His goodness and grace into your lives and marriage.

A Cord of Three Strands

Twenty-eight years ago, I looked across the room at a pastor I really didn't know, facing the complete demise of my relationship with Jody because of my great and awful sin, and came to terms with God.

Jody and I both accepted the forgiveness Jesus offers and entered into a personal relationship with Him, the same day, hour, minute and moment. I'll never forget that day as it marked the beginning of a great change in both of us that started from the inside out. As we walked out of that pastors office that night we could have never imagined all that God would do as He became our Lord, our Savior, our guide, and our hope. Jesus met us in the midst of our struggle, sin and shame. And now He is using us to encourage couples to make the necessary choices to tighten the marriage knot.

I'm writing to you not as someone with a perfect marriage, but as one who has caused self-induced hardship and yet came to the Rock, Jesus, for healing. He has become our firm foundation, and it all started with a few baby steps of faith. I want you to think about making that

> When we are finally down is when we begin to fervently look up.

choice, now, today . . . in this moment. Most importantly, have you made the choice to build your life on the rock of Jesus Christ? Have you turned to Him in repentance and faith? Can you point to a specific time in your life or a period when you accepted His work on the cross for yourself? If your answer is "no" or "I'm not sure," you can do it right now! Today is the day of salvation. Don't roll the dice on this one because eternity is at stake and it starts in this life! Maybe you're like Jody and me, struggling to build a life and marriage with someone or something else in the place of Christ. I can tell you firsthand, that's a futile approach. It will fail. You must come to the right foundation. If you want to make that decision to build your life on the Rock or recommit that decision as a couple, take a moment and pray this prayer out loud individually or together.

Dear God,

I admit that I have failed You, wronged You, and let You down. I admit that I have sinned against You as I've built my life on the sinking sand of this world. Please forgive me of my sin, as I can't stop doing the things I don't want to do. I am choosing today to build my life on the rock of who Jesus is and I desire to grow spiritually.

I believe, God, that You sent Your Son to die for me on the cross. I should have been the one who hung on that cross because of what I've done, but Jesus willingly, lovingly, and obediently took my place to pay the penalty of my sin.

I believe that Jesus rose from the grave on the third day according to the Scriptures and is seated at Your right hand.

Please help me to live the life that You have planned for me as I surrender myself to You, Jesus, as my Savior and Lord. Holy Spirit, help me, encourage me, and convict me to live a life that is pleasing to You as I invest myself more fully in God's ways and desires.

Give me a heart for Your Word and a willingness to respond to it by faith as I build my life on the rock—looking to You, leveling with You, listening to You, learning from You, and leaning on You to become the person You made me to be.

In Jesus' name, Amen.

If you prayed that prayer from the heart, I want you to know that you have made the best decision of your life—a decision that will impact every other major decision in your life. Not all at once, and seemingly not all the time, as you may not even realize the magnitude of it yet. But God has begun a new work in you that He will be faithful to complete.

The better version of yourself has just begun as the new you has become the true you. You may feel like this immense weight has been lifted, like Jody and I did, or you may just be wondering what's next.

The Bible says, "A cord of three strands is not quickly broken" (Eccl. 4:12 NIV). You and your spouse are two strands . . . Jesus Christ is the third. That's a lasting and powerful combination as you build your lives on the Rock of faith. You can move forward in boldness and faith to redeem and rebuild your lives and marriage in a way that moves you and your family closer to God and to one another.

May God be gracious to you both. And may your tribe increase.

Lovingly,

Ron and Jody

Acknowledgments

My first thanks goes most importantly to Jesus, my personal Savior and Lord, who not only rescued Jody and me, but also our marriage. Without that story, this book (and our marriage) would be nonexistent. I'm humbled that God has used our lives and story to provide hope to countless numbers of couples as they seek to build their lives and marriages on the Rock of who Jesus is.

Secondly, I'd like to thank my wonderful wife Jody, who has stayed by my side through thick and thin. Not only have you lived with me with unfailing grace through what is now the content of this book, but you've supported me each step of the way by reading each draft, giving me thoughtful feedback, and providing content for this book.

Thanks also for the patience of my wife and daughters as I worked on this book through many late nights, long car rides, and times away. Allie, Erin, and Emily, your love and support mean the world to me. I'm blessed beyond belief to be your dad and have learned so much from each of you. And now, as Josh and Allie and Steve and Erin are newly married, my hope for your marriages is by and large the content of this book—that you would learn from our experiences and build your marriages on the Rock, growing closer together as you focus on growing closer to Him.

I'd also like to thank the amazing people of Highpoint Church, who heard early versions of this content through sermons that I preached way back in 2014. That sermon series became the basis for *The Knot Marriage Conference*, and ultimately the idea for this book. A big thanks goes to our staff at Highpoint Church who have helped support me in bringing God's Word to our people each weekend, who make *The Knot Marriage Conferences* happen, and who made this book possible. Special thanks to Zack Zboncak, my assistant who labors relentlessly to make my life run easier. To Steve Smith, our executive pastor, for his faithfulness and partnership in ministry over the last ten years as well as giving me the appropriate push to get this project started. I'm grateful to God for each of you and your partnership in the gospel!

Lastly, there are a few individuals who have specifically poured into Jody and me over the years who have helped make us into who we are today: Tom Jensen (the pastor who shared the gospel with us and helped restore our marriage), and James and Kathy MacDonald (dear friends who invited us into their small group, gave us our start in ministry and have continued to support us through the decades). Thank you, sincerely from the bottom of my heart as you have taught us and modeled so much of what we have shared. Each one of you.

Small Group
Discussion Questions

Introduction

1. Using the principle of strengthening the knot of your marriage, how would you describe your marriage knot?

   - Nice and tight
   - Getting a little loose
   - Unraveling
   - Needs to be retied

2. Solomon provides a vision for a strong marriage in Ecclesiastes 4:9–12. What aspects of Solomon's description resonate most with you? What areas of your marriage need immediate attention?

3. Describe your relationship to Jesus. How would you describe your spouse's relationship to Him?

4. On a scale of 1 to 10, 10 being the highest level of motivation, how motivated are you to work on strengthening the knot of your marriage?

Chapter 1 Choose to Grow Spiritually

1. How would you describe the spiritual life of your marriage?

2. What are you doing personally to grow spiritually in your walk with the Lord?

3. How does your spouse's understanding of spiritual growth differ from yours?

4. Using the image of the Marriage Triangle, where would you place God on the triangle? Explain your answer.

5. After reading this chapter, what do you think you and your spouse need to do to strengthen your choice to grow spiritually? Any hindrances at this point? If so, can you share them with the group?

Chapter 2 Choose to Love Unconditionally

1. What struck you as most important for you personally from this chapter?

2. Based on Ron's and Jody's teaching from the Word, how would you describe unconditional love in a marriage?

3. Can you share one example where you experienced this level of love from your spouse? What were the circumstances? Try to be open and specific.

4. From the apostle Paul's list of qualities of unconditional love in 1 Corinthians 13, which do you feel need the most attention in your attitude toward your spouse?

5. What's the hardest part of loving your mate unconditionally?

Chapter 3 Choose to Serve Sacrificially

1. What did you learn from Ron and Jody in this chapter that really challenged you?

2. Was there anything in the Ephesians 5 passage that made you uncomfortable? If so, what was it and why?

3. In what ways do you feel you are sacrificing for your spouse but it's not being fully appreciated?

4. How does following Christ's example of obedience and sacrifice help transform our attitudes about loving our spouses?

5. How would you explain the idea of mutual, loving submission to one another in marriage?

Chapter 4 Choose to Please Regularly

1. How did you feel after reading this chapter? Anything make you uncomfortable? What emotions did you feel?

2. How does our culture's obsession with sex distort the Biblical concept of intimacy in marriage?

3. Why do you think couples struggle with this area of marriage?

4. What principles from Ron's and Jody's teaching helped you most in embracing this choice for marriage?

Chapter 5 **Choose to Persevere Persistently**

1. What did you learn from this chapter about the importance of perseverance in marriage?

2. How does persevering persistently relate to the marriage vows you declared to your spouse at your wedding?

3. What things challenge our ability or willingness to persevere in marriage?

4. How does your walk with the Lord enable you to make this important choice individually and as a married couple?

5. Where are you today in your commitment to persevering in your marriage? Circle the best one below:

• I'm all in no matter what

• I'm in but starting to waver

• I'm working on it but struggling

• I'm already packed . . . I'm out of here!

Chapter 6 **Choose to Communicate Respectfully**

1. What aspects of Ron's and Jody's teaching from this chapter challenged you the most?

2. What one word best describes the communication patterns in your marriage?

3. What biblical passage speaks directly to the current situation in your marriage regarding communication?

4. Would you assess the communication patterns in your marriage as *healthy* or *unhealthy*? Explain your response.

5. What is one thing you can do personally to begin to improve your communication with your spouse?

Chapter 7 Choose to Bless Abundantly

1. How often do you verbally bless your spouse?

2. What did you learn from this chapter about the importance of blessing your spouse abundantly?

3. Why do you think the concept of blessing others is so misunderstood and rarely experienced?

4. How did the Lord speak to you about the importance of making this choice as you read this chapter and reflected on His Word?

Notes

Introduction

1. Timothy Keller with Kathy Keller, *The Meaning of Marriage: Facing the Complexities of Commitment with the Wisdom of God* (New York: Penguin Books, 2016), 44.

2. Ibid., 144.

Choice #1: Choose to Grow Spiritually

1. "The Great Galveston Hurricane of 1900," NOAA, last revised May 12, 2017, https://celebrating200years.noaa.gov/magazine/galv_hurricane/welcome.html#intro.

2. "The State of the Church 2016," Barna, September 15, 2016, https://www.barna.com/research/state-church-2016/; Shaunti Feldhahn, "Busting Cultural Myths About Marriage and Divorce," Shaunti.com, https://shaunti.com/2014/05/busting-cultural-myths-marriage-divorce/.

3. Shaunti Feldhahn with Tally Whitehead, *The Good News About Marriage: Debunking Discouraging Myths about Marriage and Divorce* (Colorado Springs: Multnomah, 2014), 66.

4. Ed Stetzer, "Marriage, Divorce, and the Church: What do the stats say, and can marriage be happy?" *Christianity Today*, February 14, 2014, https://www.christianitytoday.com/edstetzer/2014/february/marriage-divorce-and-body-of-christ-what-do-stats-say-and-c.html.

5. David Stoop, "The Couple that Prays Together," Drstoop.com, August 6, 2012, http://drstoop.com/the-couple-that-prays-together/.

6. Henry Drummond, *The World's Best Orations: From the Earliest Period to the Present Time*, vol. 5 (Albany, NY: J. B. Lyon Company Printers and Binders, 1901), 1951.

7. Ronald Reagan, "Remarks at the Annual Convention of the National Religious Broadcasters," The American Presidency Project, January 30, 1984, http://www.presidency.ucsb.edu/ws/index.php?pid=40394.

Choice #4: Choose to Please Regularly

1. Lawrence B. Finer, "Trends in Premarital Sex in the United States, 1954–2003," Public Health Reports 122, no. 1 (2007): 73–78, https://www.ncbi.nlm.nih.gov/pmc/articles/PMC1802108/; Nicholas H. Wolfinger, "Counterintuitive Trends in the Link Between Premarital Sex and Marital Stability," Institute for Family Studies, June 6, 2016, https://ifstudies.org/blog/counterintuitive-trends-in-the-link-between-premarital-sex-and-marital-stability.

2. "Infidelity Statistics," http://www.siainvestigations.com/statistics/.

3. Wendy Wang, "Who Cheats More? The Demographics of Infidelity in America," Institute for Family Studies, January 10, 2018, https://ifstudies.org/blog/who-cheats-more-the-demographics-of-cheating-in-america.

4. "Infidelity Statistics," http://www.siainvestigations.com/statistics/.

5. C. S. Lewis, *Mere Christianity* (New York: Macmillan Publishing Co., 1981), 84.

6. Gary Thomas, *Sacred Marriage: What if God Designed Marriage to Make Us Holy More Than to Make Us Happy?* (Grand Rapids: Zondervan, 2000), 226.

7. http://www.standardnewswire.com/news/368369659.html.

8. For further study on this, see Mark Driscoll, *Real Marriage: The Truth About Sex, Friendship, and Life Together* (Nashville: Thomas Nelson, 2012), 178–79.

Choice #6: Choose to Communicate Respectfully

1. Gary Thomas, *Sacred Marriage: What If God Designed Marriage to Make Us Holy More Than to Make Us Happy?* (Grand Rapids: Zondervan, 2015), 154.

Choice #7: Choose to Bless Abundantly

1. David Stoop, "The Couple that Prays Together," Drstoop.com, August 6, 2012, http://drstoop.com/the-couple-that-prays-together/; see also "Marital Prayer Part 1: What Happens When a Couple Prays Together?," Doing Family Right, January 14, 2013, http://www.doingfamilyright.com/marital-prayer-part-1-what-happens-when-a-couple-prays-together/.

2. Catherine Rampell, "Money Fights Predict Divorce Rates," Economix (blog), December 7, 2009, https://economix.blogs.nytimes.com/2009/12/07/money-fights-predict-divorce-rates/.

3. http://www.wacmm.org/Stats.html.

4. Lydia Saad, "Record Few Americans Believe Bible Is Literal Word of God," Gallup, May 15, 2017, https://news.gallup.com/poll/210704/record-few-americans-believe-bible-literal-word-god.aspx.

5. Timothy Keller with Kathy Keller, *The Meaning of Marriage: Facing the Complexities of Commitment with the Wisdom of God* (New York: Penguin Books, 2016), 91.

About the Authors

Ron and Jody Zappia grew up in northeastern Ohio and met in middle school. Later becoming high school sweethearts and marrying, they entered the business world, but were on the brink of divorce in their first year of marriage. It was then when they met Jesus and their lives were transformed, ultimately leading to a life of full-time vocational ministry.

After becoming believers, Ron became a youth pastor at Harvest Bible Chapel in Rolling Meadows in 1994. After receiving his master's from Trinity Evangelical Divinity School, he and Jody were sent out and planted Highpoint Church in the spring of 2000. What started as a handful of people meeting in a basement, praying for God to move, has grown into a thriving multisite church reaching thousands each week in the western suburbs of Chicago and beyond. Pastor Ron and Jody, having come to know the Lord as adults, have a strong desire to share their faith and how Jesus can transform lives and marriages. Ron has served as the Senior Pastor of Highpoint Church since its founding.

Highpoint Ministries, the teaching ministry of Pastor Ron, launched in 2013 and includes *The Knot Marriage Conference*, daily and weekly radio broadcasts on over 500 stations around North America, podcasts, and resources available online for download and purchase.

Ron and Jody live in Wheaton, IL. They have three grown daughters: Allie, Erin, and Emily.

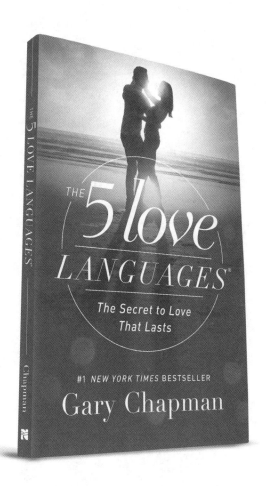

BUILD A MARRIAGE NOW THAT YOUR KIDS WILL THANK YOU FOR LATER.

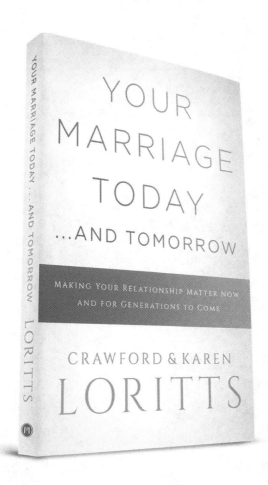

It's time to get proactive about the legacy your marriage will leave for future generations in your family. This book will teach you the biblical foundation for marriage, godly disciplines and habits that will improve your marriage, and how your marriage can shape your family's future for the better.

978-0-8024-1815-9 | also available as an eBook

BEFORE YOU PLAN YOUR WEDDING, PLAN YOUR MARRIAGE.

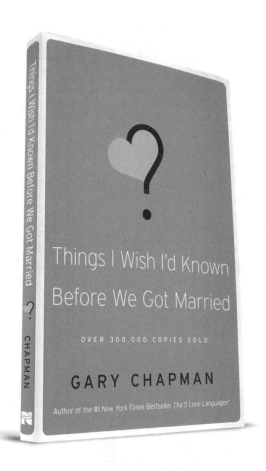